ALSO BY KAO KALIA YANG

What God Is Honored Here?
Writings on Miscarriage and Infant Loss by and for
Native Women and Women of Color
(edited with Shannon Gibney)

A Map into the World
(for children)

The Shared Room
(for children)

The Song Poet: A Memoir of My Father

The Latehomecomer: A Hmong Family Memoir

SOMEWHERE
IN THE
UNKNOWN
WORLD

SOMEWHERE
IN THE
UNKNOWN
WORLD

a collective refugee memoir

Kao Kalia Yang

METROPOLITAN BOOKS

HENRY HOLT AND COMPANY

NEW YORK

Metropolitan Books
Henry Holt and Company
Publishers since 1866
120 Broadway
New York, New York 10271
www.henryholt.com

Library of Congress Cataloging-in-Publication Data

Names: Yang, Kao Kalia, 1980– author.
Title: Somewhere in the unknown world : a collective refugee memoir /
    Kao Kalia Yang.
Description: First edition. | New York : Metropolitan Books,
    Henry Holt and Company, [2020]
Identifiers: LCCN 2020002964 (print) | LCCN 2020002965 (ebook) |
    ISBN 9781250296856 (trade paperback) | ISBN 9781250296863
    (ebook)
Subjects: LCSH: Refugees—United States. | Immigrants—United States. |
    United States—Emigration and immigration—Social aspects.
Classification: LCC HV640.4 .U54 Y364 2020 (print) | LCC HV640.4
    .U54 (ebook) | DDC 305.9/06914092273—dc23
LC record available at https://lccn.loc.gov/2020002964
LC ebook record available at https://lccn.loc.gov/2020002965

Our books may be purchased in bulk for promotional, educational,
or business use. Please contact your local bookseller or the Macmillan
Corporate and Premium Sales Department at (800) 221-7945, extension
5442, or by e-mail at MacmillanSpecialMarkets@macmillan.com.

First Edition 2020

Designed by Meryl Sussman Levavi

Printed in the United States of America

1 3 5 7 9 10 8 6 4 2

For the refugees from everywhere—men, women, and children whose fates have been held by the interests of nations, whose rights have been contested and denied, whose thirst and hunger go unheeded and unseen.

quilting

somewhere in the unknown world
a yellow eyed woman
sits with her daughter
quilting.

some other where
alchemists mumble over pots.
their chemistry stirs
into science. their science
freezes into stone.

in the unknown world
the woman
threading together her need
and her needle
nods toward the smiling girl
remember
this will keep us warm.

how does this poem end?
   do the daughters' daughters quilt?
   do the alchemists practice their tables?
   do the worlds continue spinning
   away from each other forever?

—LUCILLE CLIFTON

Contents

Part IV: Edge of the Horizon

Prologue

I was born a stateless Hmong girl in Ban Vinai Refugee Camp in Thailand. For the first six years of my life, I understood that the camp was only our holding center. We lived in the third sector, in the third subdivision, in room six, a small sleeping quarter I shared with my mother, father, and older sister. From the moment of my birth, the people who loved me told me that it was not my home. Home was once the tall mountains on the other side of the river. Home would one day be some foreign country on the other side of the ocean.

I had not experienced war myself, but I was surrounded by its consequences. The adults around me told me stories of what had happened in Laos. On the hot days when the sun blazed in the blue sky, beneath the shade of thatched roofs, I traced the scars on the adults I loved, ripples of rising skin, sunken flesh where bones should be. I knew their different cries in the dark of night, the nightmares from which they fought to surface each morning, the tired, empty look in their eyes, and the fear in me that perhaps the people I loved were broken inside. On paper, I was a refugee.

I looked the part. I was small for my age, thin and short, had big round eyes that peeked at the world from beneath my bangs with suspicious curiosity. I was a little creature, kept in a little cage. I was a child keenly aware of the dangers of a world in which I belonged to no nation.

When my family came to America and I was sent to school, I was placed in a class with many other refugee children, mostly Hmong like myself, but also Cambodian and Vietnamese. I was one of the youngest in a mixed-aged class. During art, some of the big students drew pictures of things they had seen before coming to America. A tall boy with watery eyes drew a picture of a thick green jungle, and then a single foot sticking out onto a dirt path. The foot looked heavy and stiff and blue, like a stone statue of a foot. The boy said that the foot belonged to his brother. He'd found his brother after an ambush. He hadn't had the courage to look into the heavy brush, to see if his brother's body was intact, to look at his face. The older children who had seen more than we had wanted to let their stories out, for us younger ones to carry the weight of their memories together with them. We were willing because they were like our older brothers and sisters, our mothers and fathers, aunts and uncles—all those who'd lived through the wars.

I have carried the stories of those around me all my life. I never thought that I would write them down, and I wouldn't have had my grandmother not died illiterate and fearful that the journey she had traveled in her life would be forgotten. So I told a story that much of America did not know, about a people who were new to the written form. Traveling across the country to speak about my book, from state to state, city to city, I met many refugee resettlement workers and refugees. I discovered how little we knew of each other's lives and how the isolating loneliness many of us felt was a shared experience.

Other refugees asked me to tell their stories, but I wasn't

ready. I was a young writer then, looking for legitimacy in literary America, in a genre dominated by white authors. I was struggling to build confidence and stand up for the Hmong and I could not fathom how I would carry the stories of other people. But, even then, I was bearing witness to the heartache and the yearning of refugee men and women wanting to be understood.

Over the past few years, I could not fail to see an America that was questioning its long history of refugee resettlement, an America that seeks to define itself by casting its vulnerable immigrants and incoming refugees to the margins of society. Greater than my fear of what I could not do was a growing need to convey the refugee lives around me, to show our shared understanding of war and hunger for peace, our vulnerabilities and strengths, and to offer our powerful truths to a country I love.

◆

When the cold comes to Minnesota, it arrives quickly. On an October evening, the air feels particularly balmy. The colorful leaves of autumn sway in the dark wind and the moon, a sliver of a fingernail, hangs low in the heavens. Then, the next day, the world feels different. The air has turned crisp, and the soft yielding grass of yesterday is gone and covered with frost.

I have lived in Minnesota for more than thirty-two years. I understand the process of the changing seasons well enough. But even with this knowledge, each cycle of fall becoming winter strikes me as something new. My heart is never quite ready for the frigid wind that will seep through my clothes, skin, flesh, and bone. Without central heating, insulated walls, the buffer of a jacket, hat, scarf, and mittens, I won't survive. Winter is humbling in Minnesota.

Winter here prepared me for the work of writing this book.

The endless days of gray gave me ample opportunity to reflect on my own journey and see that this once stateless child is here in Minnesota telling stories because I walked a broad margin of possibility; I met extraordinary people who gave me the gift of their experiences, which shaped my understanding and informed my conscience.

This book is an endeavor of the heart. I listened to each of the people represented here and then processed their stories slowly. I made a promise to myself: I would tell the story of every person I spoke to. I'd too often witnessed members of my family and community recount their experiences, weeping as they returned to their past, only to have it live and die in the moment because the listeners deemed other stories more important. I didn't want to be that person. I then wrote each chapter, weaving in research to fill in the areas of the world I've never been to, and then sent it on to the interviewee with a direct question, "Is the story accurate?" In the hopeful corners of my heart, I dream that *Somewhere in the Unknown World* will be received as an expression of my admiration for the individuals revealed here and that their stories will be helpful to their families and communities.

Somewhere in the Unknown World takes place in Minnesota, my home state. There are refugees from everywhere here, from wars past and present. In fact, the state is home to more refugees per capita than any other state in the nation. We have the highest concentration of Hmong and Tibetan in the country, the biggest populations of Somali, Karen, Burmese, Eritrean, and Liberian refugees. This much is known, but few know who we are or how we live. There are worlds within worlds, possibilities not visible, individuals who struggle and survive the unimaginable every day to be here.

SOMEWHERE
IN THE
UNKNOWN
WORLD

Part I

OTHER PEOPLE'S CHILDREN

1

From Irina to Irene

ANY PASSERBY CAN tell you that Irina has dark hair and dark eyes, but if you look carefully at her, you'll see that Irina's thick hair is a deep auburn and that her eyes are a blend of brown and green—like gardens of kelp beds and seagrass meadows.

Irina was ten years old. She was excited about the coming New Year, her favorite holiday.

Underneath the bed she shared with her older sister, Edith, there were four bananas ripening. Each year, Papa received them as a bonus from the trucking company he worked for as a mechanical engineer. They were the only bananas the family got all year. The coming of the bananas was an occasion of pride and joy for the whole family. It was always with great ceremony that Papa unveiled the bananas from his work bag. They were green and hard. Mama would grab a small basket from the kitchen, line it with a white towel, and then carefully place the bananas side by side. Papa placed the basket underneath the girls' bed and told them they were in charge of the ripening process.

Edith was less keen on observing the bananas, but Irina took the job seriously. She knew from prior years that the ripening process for bananas is very specific: a green banana will first turn yellow with green tips before it turns completely yellow. If you don't eat it immediately, its smell will grow sugary and strong, small brown spots will form on the banana's skin. From the point Papa placed the bananas underneath the bed, Irina knew the family had four or five days until they were perfectly ripe for eating.

Every night, the sweet scent of the bananas kept Irina up imagining the big day when the whole family would gather around the dining table to celebrate the new year and savor the delicious fruit. The thought of the bananas made her mouth wet with saliva. To distract herself, she thought about her birthday in March. Mama did not like to make a big deal of birthdays, but she allowed the girls to make just a little deal. Irina knew that Mama would get her a white dress to wear on her birthday. Irina fell asleep dreaming about the white dress and the sweetness of bananas.

It was Mama who woke the girls up each morning, opening their door, poking her head in, dark hair pulled back into a clean bun. "Girls, it is time to get up!"

The first thing Irina did each morning was check on the bananas underneath the bed. The sight of the yellow fruits brought on the morning cheer, wiping the sleep from her eyes. Irina's smile revealed small white teeth, spaced slightly apart, dimples on either side of her face. She reached out her hand and gently brushed the bananas before attending to her morning routine.

When it was finally time for 1989 to begin, Irina was jittery with excitement. On New Year's Eve, the whole of their family gathered around the dining table in their crowded kitchen: Mama, Papa, Edith, and Irina, their grandma and grandpa, their beloved aunt and uncle, and their cousins. Mama and the rest of the women put a colorful feast on the table. In a glass bowl there was beet salad—a mix of sauerkraut, boiled beets in deep, dark magenta, diced with white beans in a tangy vinaigrette. There was a platter of small pieces of buttered white bread with gray caviar, a symbol of hope for the new year. There were saucers of pickled cucumbers and mushrooms. Irina's aunt had made meat pies, beautifully browned in her oven at home. In the middle of the table, on a big platter, there was *kholodets*, meat jelly, and a side of grated horseradish. The bananas were always saved for dessert.

Papa cut them up into chunks. The children got first pick. Irina held the peeled banana up to her mouth. She could eat the whole thing in one big bite or take tiny nibbles and spend her time savoring the long-awaited treat like she knew Edith would. Irina smiled her naughty smile and opened her mouth wide. She chewed with full cheeks and then slowly swallowed it down. She took a careful sip of sparkling lemonade. The adults drank champagne. Every year, Edith and Irina led their little cousins over to their grandma and grandpa, and all four stuck out their tongues. Grandma and Grandpa took turns pouring bits of champagne for the children to taste. The taste was more bitter than sweet. The girls made faces, and everyone laughed.

The apartment was filled with photographs of old relatives, of Mama and Papa when they were younger, of Edith and Irina as little children in stiff-looking dresses with big collars, the good times the family had shared. That night the apartment was ringing with the noise from the television show *Novogodniy Goluboy Ogonek, New Year's Little Blue Light*. The children loved the festive lights and the sparkling trees on the television screen. Irina was especially moved by the music the orchestra played. When the adults on the television held hands and danced in a circle, the four cousins followed suit. When the pretty lady with red lipstick held a microphone and started singing, it was only Irina who held her hand in front of her mouth and sang along.

Irina had no idea that this would be her last New Year's celebration in Minsk.

The Jewish students had been disappearing from school for years. They never said much about where they were going or why, so their fellow students gave little thought to their departures. There were students whom Irina and Edith didn't even know were Jewish until they vanished; when they were gone, all the children would laugh and say it like a joke. "Oh, they're Jewish, too."

Shortly after the new year, on another cold evening, Irina's parents, aunt, uncle, and grandparents gathered around the dining table and talked about how there were so few opportunities for Jewish people in Belarus.

Mama said, "I want Edith and Irina to go to college and get jobs."

Grandma said, "I worry about their basic rights."

Papa said nothing.

Papa's whole family had been killed in the Holocaust. He did not talk about them often, let alone mention how they were killed. When Irina had wanted to ask in the past, Mama had said in a hushed whisper, "It's too painful for Papa. Leave the questions be. It is enough to know that everyone was killed."

Uncle said, "The family beside our apartment are leaving soon."

Aunt said, "When are we going to leave?"

She added, "What are we waiting for?"

They talked about Mama's cousin who had left in the 1970s and how their lives were going well in America. They talked about a plan.

As the adults talked, Irina sat with her young cousins nearby, reading *The Adventures of Pippi Longstocking* aloud in Russian. The girls were a captive audience and Pippi was Irina's favorite character in any book, so the adults' conversation served as little more than background noise.

It was a week before Irina's birthday when Mama and Papa came into the girls' bedroom as they were preparing for bed. A single lamp lit up the small room.

Mama and Papa sat on the bed and said, "Girls, we are leaving Minsk soon."

One or the other said, "Don't tell anyone at school."

The plan was indeed a simple one: like the other Jewish children, Edith and Irina would also just disappear with their family.

Irina thought about how her disappearance would not be a big deal because she was just a student, but Mama's would be. Mama taught English and teachers did not just vanish in the middle of a school year unless they had babies or were deathly ill or had family emergencies. Irina felt bad that Mama's students would not be able to continue studying with Mama. She was a good teacher, stern but precise, just as she was as a mother.

Later, when the lamp had been turned off and Edith had turned her back to find sleep, Irina grew excited at the possibility of leaving Minsk behind. It was going to be the first adventure of her life. She was finally going to be like Pippi. She, Irina, was going to see and experience the world. She wondered if she would be like Russian royalty and eat peeled sunflower seeds in a new country. Irina decided that wherever the family ended up, she would eat bananas every day. She fell asleep smiling, listening to the quiet of the city, feeling the cocoon of winter around her.

On March 18, Irina's birthday, no one remembered. She waited all day for someone to say something or do something, for a gift to be presented, but nothing happened. Everybody ran around packing the things they could not imagine living without. By day's end, Irina's eyes were pools of liquid waiting to spill. It was Mama who finally saw, and said to Irina, "Follow me."

In her parents' room, a mess of open drawers and small packages, Mama riffled through her top dresser drawer. She turned around and handed Irina a little bag, a gift to cheer her youngest daughter on her eleventh birthday. Irina opened the little bag with trembling hands. She had been sure she was going to get a dress. What was this?

Inside the little bag was a blue glass bottle with a small gold chain linking its neck to its golden cap. On the bottle was the prettiest flower, a red flower that looked like a tulip at the bottom, but whose petals opened like a rose on top. The gift was so delicate. Irina held it close to her nose. The smell that wafted up into her nose was like the image of the flower on the bottle, a combination of different blooms she couldn't place.

Irina held the perfume to her flat chest, feeling for the first time in her life like a woman.

That night, Irina went to bed thinking about a faraway country. She saw herself as a grown woman. The woman in her dreams was small but beautiful: dark hair, dark eyes, the same naughty smile, a slimming dress, high heels, a microphone in her hands and a song on her lips.

On the evening of March 20, 1989, a bus came in the middle of the night to take the family on their great adventure. The family of four would travel with the grandparents, aunt, uncle, and little cousins. On the bus, Irina held her copy of *Pippi Longstocking* in her lap. The moon was hidden by dark clouds in the sky. The night air was cold. It was late March, but all around there were still bits of snow.

The border agents didn't care that more Jewish families were leaving the former Soviet Union. They were happy to see them go. Throughout the country's history, there had always been times when the borders would open for Jewish people to leave. Each family was given two hundred rubles and each person was allowed to take two suitcases out of the country. They asked only that the families leave in the dark of night so appearances could be maintained.

From the border, the family took a fancy train to Warsaw on which Edith and Irina had an entire car to themselves, including beds and a bathroom. The trip lasted only an hour. By the time they reached the capital city, the world was still shrouded in night. The city was asleep, with closed businesses and empty streets; Irina has never forgotten that the whole of the city smelled like bread.

In the yeasty city, the family stood on a street corner outside the train station and talked about an organization called HIAS, a group which would be taking care of them until they reached their final destination.

Irina asked, "Is HIAS very expensive, Papa?"

"No, Irina. You don't worry about it."

All the adults treated Irina like a girl at the beginning of the journey. No one could have guessed how quickly she would grow up.

From Warsaw, the family took another train to Austria. This time, the car was so full of people there was little seating available. Only the youngest children got to take turns lying across their mother's lap. Mama and Papa decided that Edith and Irina were no longer young children, so they spent most of the time standing.

In Vienna, the family met springtime in a cacophony of birdsong and tulips in bloom. The stores were full of ripe bananas and everyone got one to eat. Irina savored this first full banana, peeling the thick skin, taking first one measured bite, then another.

Their last stop was Rome. Upon the family's arrival at the hotel where they were staying, Mama told both girls to change into their best clothes immediately.

She said, "We have to run to an appointment, girls."

Irina put on her white birthday dress from the year before, as planned.

Mama, Papa, Edith, and Irina raced to the appointment across a city that felt like a palace. At the appointment, Mama and Papa signed paperwork, showed documents, and answered questions. Edith and Irina waited on hard wooden chairs. At first, Irina thought the cramps were the result of nerves. When they didn't end, but worsened, she started whimpering.

Edith whispered, "What's wrong?"

All Irina could say was, "I ate the banana too fast. It does not agree with me."

By the time the appointment was through, Irina was almost crying with pain. Mama and Papa raced the girls back across the expansive squares and the spread of decorated buildings.

Every few minutes, Mama assured Irina, "We're almost home."

Home was a cramped, uncomfortable hotel room in a basement. Home consisted of twin beds and a small bathroom the whole family shared. At home, Mama instructed Irina to go to the bathroom and sit on the toilet to see if the cramps would go away.

In the bathroom, Irina discovered blood on her underpants.

She screamed, "I'm dying!"

Mama ran to the bathroom and opened the door. Between Irina's knees, she could see the once white underpants now smeared with bright red.

"Oh, God, no," she said.

She ran back out of the room, closing the door behind her.

Minutes ticked by. Sweat dribbled down Irina's face. Cramps continued in waves low in her belly. She prayed again and again, "Please don't let me die in Rome."

Irina waited with a pounding heart until Mama came back. Mama was now measured and calm. After she closed the door to the bathroom behind her, she handed Irina thick white pads.

She said, "This will take care of it. It's natural for girls who are growing up to get their monthly period."

Irina's knees started shaking. She felt relief flow through her body, and then laughter climbing her throat. Her fear turned into joy in a fast minute. This was perfect. Not only was her life changing, but her body would no longer be the same.

Later that night at dinner in the hotel restaurant, beneath an old chandelier, with dust motes floating about them, Grandma walked to Irina's chair, bowed low to her ear, and whispered, "I hope this part of your life goes as smoothly and well as mine did. Welcome to womanhood, Irina."

In response to the warmth of her words, Irina blushed and looked at her hands.

Grandma kissed Irina with the gentlest of kisses, a touch of lips on her ear.

Irina looked up and Grandma winked.

With the arrival of her period, her family started treating Irina differently. In the twin bed they shared, Edith told her jokes and giggled. When Irina asked where they were headed next, Mama and Papa did not tell her "Not to worry." Instead, they said, "We will have to wait for our paperwork to be processed here in Italy." Instead of asking more persistent questions as she would have done in Minsk, Irina responded with "Okay."

Russian Jews were flooding into the country. Many of them, exhausted from the clamor of Rome, had found work taking care of gorgeous villas in surrounding cities and towns. Aunt and Uncle had found two beautiful villas for themselves and Mama and Papa to take care of while the wealthy owners were away. Irina tucked her beloved *Pippi* away in the suitcase for good when the family left Rome for the seaside resort town where they stayed the rest of their time as refugees.

Santa Marinella was the first place where Irina experienced the beauties of being a woman. Santa Marinella, located north of Rome, on the coast, was as far away from Minsk as she could imagine. The ocean lapped at the beaches like the tongue of a thirsty dog at a pool of water. Blue umbrellas lined the edge of the sea as people in bathing suits basked in the sun. Palm trees stood proudly from the high cliffs and between houses like old men in the uniforms of their youth. In Santa Marinella, Irina saw women enjoying life, relaxing, taking deep breaths of sea breeze, letting down their hair, and spreading their arms high over their head to feel the wonder of the world.

The family settled in a sprawling estate. Its gate was ringed with tropical palms and its driveway curved up to the front of a grand house the color of white sand. The house sat like a jewel with shiny windows glinting in the sun, in a sea of emerald-green grass.

Inside, as the family's voices echoed against the cool marble stairwell and the high curve of the ceiling, Mama said, "You can't lean on anything. Not the furniture, the walls, the pillars, the stair rails, anything."

Mama added, "Pretend like you were never here."

Edith, Papa, and Irina walked on their toes on the spotless marble floor to minimize any footprints. They talked in whispers as they went from one room to the next, each with a tall window that allowed a view of the sea and the sky in equal measure. They laughed quietly about how they would be shadows of themselves in the luxurious villa overlooking the sea. The sound of the waves came in through the windows and walls and greeted their laughter.

Irina's aunt and uncle's villa was not far and the families visited often. Occasionally, Irina made the trip by herself, feeling independent and safe.

On the way, Irina passed other villas with gardens, sometimes cultured, but other times overgrown, wild, and in her opinion more beautiful. On the path, there was an abandoned amusement park: old cement garden gnomes stood like guards among unchecked vines that grew over the old rides, rusted metal roasting in the hot sun. There were even fountains full of green things growing where water once ran. The park was full of strange creatures made out of cement, metal, marble, and other materials that Irina did not know. Each time she passed the amusement park, the girl from Minsk wondered what it would have been like to go on the rides, even as the young woman she was becoming felt a wave of sadness and sorrow for the abandoned place, the things that are left behind.

The family stayed in Italy for three months, as spring turned to summer. Time moved slowly in that place of the sun, but that waiting period gave Irina time and space to remember and to forget what it had been like to be a girl and to encounter the beginnings of womanhood. Irina grew accustomed to a changing body, the swell of her breasts, the widening of her hips. In the spotless mirror of the fancy house, Irina saw that even her face had changed. Its previous roundness was disappearing and the bones of her mother's face were peeking through.

Every evening, all the refugees congregated on the beach to talk about the news. Hundreds of Russian Jews met up on the smooth, white sand in their fine clothes. They were all part of an exodus. The adults stood together and told the older children to watch over the younger ones so they would not wander too far into the sea. Each night, the family found that some of their friends had left, while new ones had come to fill their place. The wind and the ocean beckoned as the large gathering stood in uncertain freedom, tethered to shared histories and places far away. Among them, Irina stood fast, smelling like perfume, staring out toward the future.

Every night on the beach the group found out who was going where, who got accepted and who got denied. There was always some family talking about how they'd been waiting for over a year to get processed. Many offered tips. It was a bad idea to say you were members of the Communist Party. It was not a good idea to say that your life had been easy, that you were an excellent student, or that you had been well respected at work. No one said anyone should lie, of course. But if you wanted to do well at the interviews, and each family usually went through two or three interviews before being accepted for resettlement, you had to say that you lived in the long shadow of Russian Jewish history, that your people had survived pogroms, and that you were the remnants. The world knew what had happened to the Jews in Russia, but it did not know what would happen to the Jews now. Irina's family was part of that not-knowing.

Mama was tense about the interviews. She was mad at Papa for being so proud of his work as a mechanical engineer in Minsk. She did not like that Edith, contrary to advice, talked of her good grades and her friends. Irina did not talk. Instead, she sat quietly in the now too small white dress. However, as the best one at English, Mama did most of the speaking at the interviews, so the family was accepted to the United States.

There were options. A family could choose to go to New York City for free, a place full of Jews from around the world, a place full of most of the world. There was also Los Angeles, although that was more expensive as each family would have to pay two hundred dollars per person up front for the paperwork. If a family wanted to go anywhere else, they needed sponsors. Mama had cousins who had gone to a state called Minnesota, and they agreed to sponsor Irina's family.

Minnesota was not a part of America that was famous. Irina had never thought to look it up on a map. All she knew was what Mama and Papa said.

"Minnesota's weather is a lot like Minsk's. The winters are cold but the summers are temperate."

"There are some Russian Jews there so we would not be the first. They've done well, so we will, too."

Aunt and Uncle, Grandma and Grandpa, and the cousins chose to go to Los Angeles. It was only in those final days in Italy that the family, afraid to speak of the imminent separation, spoke about what they had left behind in Minsk.

Irina's family would be leaving the warm coastal city. They didn't know that they would be on welfare after HIAS helped them pay for their first year in the new country. They didn't know that they would have to be prepared to live on five hundred dollars a month as a family of four. Mama would become a babysitter and Papa a pizza delivery guy. Irina couldn't have known that her auburn hair and brown-green eyes would help her fit in as an American. Irina would be changed to Irene.

When the family packed for America, Irina folded away the white dress. She tucked her copy of *Pippi Longstocking* inside it, knowing that she had outgrown both. The bottle of perfume in its little bag she placed in a corner of her luggage. She reminded herself that when she thought she was dying, she was only beginning a new life. Irina closed her suitcase firmly.

In America, Irene learned how to turn her memories and feelings into songs, songs in Russian, that say life is the beautiful moment. She allowed the weight of the memories, the leaving and the letting go, to enter into her voice so it became as full of the past as it was of the present.

A year after they left Minsk, in cold Minnesota, beneath another dark sky, Irene celebrated her twelfth birthday. The family planned a real birthday party. Mama bought a black dress and Edith put silver lipstick on her lips. The apartment the family lived in was decorated with balloons that hung from the ceiling. There was a cake, frosted with sugar that melted on the tongue. Irene laughed with the friends she had made during the year of calling Minnesota home—blond Sarah; Felicia, an African American; Kim and Linh, who were Vietnamese American; and Dina and Julie, who were Russian and had also left Minsk behind. The girls wore birthday party hats and stood around the dining table where there was a small dish of sunflower seeds next to a bowlful of ripe bananas.

—IRENE RUDERMAN CLARK

2

The Strongest Love Story

Awo knows that her mother and father love each other.
How else could they have survived these twenty years, talking
on the phone only on Saturdays, if they didn't love each other,
were not devoted to the family they have built across oceans,
not united in the most holy of marriages?

Maryam, Awo's mother, had been a nurse. She met Awo's
father, a man ten years older, a doctor, in the big hospital in the
capital city of Mogadishu. The two fell in love. They got married. They had Awo. The family lived a good life before news
of the war reached them and propelled them out of the city
they shared, back to the places they were from.

Awo's mother was a daughter of Buuhoodle, a city in the
middle of Somalia, the plains of the country, a place full of red
soil so soft and dry that Awo knew it to be as valuable as saf-
fron. Her father was a son of Laascaanood, a city set against a
backdrop of gentle, rolling hills, where lonely trees stand tall
across the landscape. Between her mother and father, there
were 98.2 miles of road, a journey that took three hours and
nine minutes in a good car.

When the couple left Mogadishu, Awo's mother and father
also left behind their years of being together in the same place as

husband and wife. Awo, just a toddler, tethered to her mother, left her father behind. The two decided that it was safer for Awo's father to work in his home village far away from the quiet place his wife came from, where their children would grow up. They understood that in a war, there was no knowing who would visit a doctor and if a doctor could save a life or not; there was no knowing the consequences of dire situations. During the worst of the war years, they further decided that a quiet village would not be safe enough; Awo's mother took the children to Kenya. From Kenya, they left for America. Thus, Awo's mother and father's marriage was a union separated at first by miles of road and then the spread of oceans; their children were the hands that stretched helplessly across that distance.

◆

The only memories Awo has of the war come to her in a continuous nightmare. In the dream, Awo is a child again.

I am a little girl with an oval face, emphasized by my hijab. I have big, round eyes, a small nose, a fine chin. The adults think I'm like a doll, a picture of cuteness. I like the way they see me. I am so young that I also like the way I see myself.

I stand in a courtyard. The walls around me are painted white. There's a bright sun shining down. It is almost noon because the sun is on top of me and my shadow is short and squat. There is a heavy wind blowing. My hijab spreads out around me. My gray shadow is a more magical creature than human, a changing thing moving in different directions. I lift my arms. I have wings. Like a bird, I fly around and around the courtyard.

I hug the hard, smooth skin of the palm tree in front of me. I see that there is a matching one on the other side of the yard. My little girl arms wrap themselves around the thick trunk. The tree feels alive, warm, fleshy, but too firm to be flesh. My hold is tight around the tree, my fingers meeting on the other side. I'm clinging. I realize that I'm afraid. My feelings are suddenly confused.

I notice that there are two guard dogs running around the compound. They both have their yellow eyes on me. Their bodies are black. Their nails sharp. They walk toward me, their tails raised high. Their ears are pointy triangles in the air. Their mouths are open, teeth glistening white. They are snarling at me. I can hear the wind from their throats.

I look around and try to find safety. All the adults are gathered in a corner of the compound. They stand with their heads bowed beneath the shade of a tall tree, its mushroom canopy casting a shadow over them.

I can see an aunt standing at the edge of the group. Her hands are held to her face. She is crying. Grief is pouring out of her body like a bucket tipped over. I can make out her cries, louder than the dogs' snarls. She is my target for protection.

I run for her.

The dogs run for me.

We chase each other, around and around in a figure eight. They run like circus dogs, trained to follow each other, so it looks like a child's game to the adults. The grown-ups cannot tell how afraid I am. They are not even looking at me. When I run out of breath and I feel my feet slipping, I know I will crash to the ground. I can feel the pounding of my blood coursing through my veins, I can see the splatter of red on the ground once the fangs of the hungry dogs penetrate my skin. I make a noise, part squeak and part scream.

My aunt's arms are around me. She lifts me high. The dogs back slowly away. My arms are tight around my aunt's neck. I make sure the dogs are no longer a danger before I look at her face. Her brown skin is wet with streams of tears. My fingers, small and slender, move to stem the flow of wet on her face. Her skin is smooth. I let my hands skim along the surface of her wet skin, follow the wet streaks from her eyes, all the way down to her chin, until I touch her scarf. Her scarf is damp. I look around me as if waking from a dream.

All the adults around me are crying, eyes trained to the base of the tree. All of a sudden, I hear their sniffles, wails, hiccups, blowing noses, swallowed cries. I shift around in the arms holding me. I can feel the stiffness of her hold, then hesitance, and then give. I see the rectangle of dug earth in the ground, the pile of the red and yellow dirt of Mogadishu by its side. I see the open coffin, the rigid body of my uncle inside it, his eyes closed to the brightness of the day, his face as gray as the remnants of last night's fire in the dawn.

Night after night, Awo wakes up from this dream. Her fear of the dogs is not enough to wake her but the sorrow evoked by the still figure of her uncle does.

She sits up in her single bed by the wall. She can hear the steady breathing of her sisters in their full bed by the other wall. Between the two beds, there's a small space of carpet, big enough for a slim body to walk through. Awo calms her racing heart by mirroring the breaths of her sleeping sisters, in then out, in then out. Her stiff body softens once she is conscious of the even rise and fall of her chest. She lies back down.

The room is dark and full of sleep. Her sisters' breathing is rhythmic and deep. Awo knows she will have to get up and prepare for the day soon. The family will go to the mosque and commune with other Somali people, eat and talk, listen and learn, and pray. Sunday will run by in a rush and then it will be Monday again. Another week of school awaits. Wait. It is summertime now. They don't have school. Instead, Awo has her internship at the medical clinic in Edina. She gets paid a real check every two weeks. Although only a sophomore in high school, Awo helps her mother take care of her younger siblings now. Awo shakes her head to clear away the remains of the dream.

Awo reaches for her phone, tucked beneath her soft pillow. She presses a button and the screen lights up. A photograph of her mother smiling appears. It's only three in the morning. Awo goes online. She visits YouTube and looks for a video of the sound of ocean waves hitting the beach. The weight of the phone on her chest, Awo keeps her body straight but turns her head toward the wall. She wiggles her right foot out from under the comforter so that it touches the cool wall. She closes her eyes, and the sound of the ocean lulls Awo to sleep once again; she has no memories of visiting the sea, despite having been born in Mogadishu, a coastal city—she left too early to remember.

In the morning, in their small kitchen, her mother is making fresh *kimis*, rolling out dough, cooking the circles of flat dough on a pan. Awo stands before the stove and uses a spatula to flip the flat bread sizzling in olive oil. She mentions the recurring dream to her mother. The woman in the brown hijab is moving quickly, the circles of dough ready for the pan stacking up in front of her, but Awo knows she is listening. When the last ball of dough is flattened, she wipes her hands on a dish towel and says, "That is not a dream, Awo. That dream comes from your life. The courtyard you described was our house in Mogadishu. Those were our dogs, and the funeral, that funeral was the funeral of your uncle."

Awo wants to ask her mother more questions but there is no time and she is more concerned about the older woman than her own curiosity. She does not want to revive the old hurts. Awo knows the answers will make her mother sad. She knows how hard her mother tries not to be sad in front of her and her siblings. It is too early in the day for tears. Awo can't bear the thought of ever causing her mother pain.

The younger siblings enter the kitchen and living area one by one, first the sisters and then the brothers. Everyone situates themselves at the round table. The tea kettle on the stove lets out its morning whistle. Awo moves quickly to prepare the family's morning tea carefully, her tapered fingers and slender hands dancing in the air as she moves between the kettle and the cups.

At the table, Awo serves cups of hot tea for everyone. The family passes around olive oil and a jar of honey. Awo's favorite way to eat morning *kimis* is to spread olive oil on the bread and then dribble it with honey. She rolls the spongey bread on her plate and then eats delicately, taking sips of hot tea with milk in between bites. There is a quiet in the apartment in the mornings. Awo savors the calm and makes a firm decision to let go of the dream.

On the bus to Edina, Awo finds herself trying to remember the last time her mother cried.

The family's journey away from Somalia is a story Awo knows only in bits and pieces. Memories play in her mind like scenes from a silent movie, with a simultaneous time line that moves toward her mother's past and her own future, both shrouded in mystery.

It was hot in Nairobi, Kenya. The family had been in the country for several years. Maryam was only in her early thirties and pregnant when she'd arrived with her three oldest children. Her youngest wasn't even conceived yet.

The children saw the city only from their rooftop apartment. Awo has no memories of making her way through the busy streets below.

Her maternal grandmother hung laundry to dry on the clotheslines strung across the rooftop. The colorful hijabs and the white cotton *macawiis* flapped in the wind like sails. Awo and her younger brother Mohamed played a game between the hanging sheets. Beneath the hot sun, the damp sheets were cool. The children laughed as they chased each other up and down the lines of clothes, caught up in the magic of their world sandwiched between the expanse of sky and cement.

Awo was chasing Mohamed. He ran between the sheets, from one end of the rooftop to the other. He was leaping like a gazelle. Awo chased as fast as she could. He grabbed on to a metal rod at the edge of the cement wall that kept the children safe from a long fall. A sheet blew into Awo's face. She shoved it aside with both hands—in time to see the metal rod turn and her eight-year-old brother swing off the roof. He held fast, his legs kicking at the air below. Neither of them made a sound. Then Awo heard the sound of the rod breaking. Mohamed flew before her eyes. She jumped after him, her hands cutting through air toward the boy who had become a blur of legs. She caught his ankle, one ankle in both hands. The young girl braced a bare foot against the cement wall and pulled. Awo swayed with the weight of her brother and felt her arms grow taut as she held tight with all the strength of her ten-year-old body and prayed to Allah. Mohamed's chin connected with the hard side of the building as Awo pulled him back onto the roof. Blood and tears soaked his face. Once she had wrestled him over the edge, she pulled him close to her neck, both of them too stunned to make a sound. Awo thanked Allah for her name that day; Awo means "lucky" in the Somali language.

The two siblings stood on that roof shaking with their luck.

Below them, on the street, the people were poor. Kenya was a kind country that had opened its doors to many of its African neighbors whose countries were ravaged by war and death. Its city streets were teeming with impoverished people in despair.

Awo and Mohamed were not poor children. They were the children of professionals. They, the three oldest, had a special tutor who visited their apartment each weekday to help prepare them with English lessons, for their lives across the ocean. Beyond their education, they were well fed, unlike many of the children who wandered the streets. Each night they slept in the safety of their apartment, cognizant of other children on the streets below. They did not know that some of those children found sleep each night only when they had placed heavy stones or bricks across their thin, shriveled bellies to quiet the cries for food in the darkened alleys of the city. Awo and Mohamed knew they were the fortunate ones, even in light of the near-death experience Mohamed had just survived.

Awo dried Mohamed's tears with gentle fingers. They held each other as they made their way into the apartment, his head resting awkwardly on her thin shoulder; the boy was nearly as tall as his sister despite a difference in age of two years. The pair took careful steps across the hot rooftop, now caught in roles they'd not quite envisioned. He clutched her middle tight. Awo felt like her mother; she had saved a life.

While Awo's mother hardly ever talked of the past, she carried herself as someone in the business of saving lives. She split her time taking care of the youngest girls, the little girl she'd given birth to in Kenya and then the new arrival, conceived during one of the rare visits from Awo's father, and thinking of a plan for the future. She was concerned, because the new babies were not included in the original paperwork when the family had first entered Kenya and registered as refugees of war. When the applications were approved, Awo's mother faced a devastating decision: to come to America with her three oldest and leave her two youngest behind, or to stay in Kenya and try to attain paperwork for the two new ones—knowing their presence would be challenging to explain in the context of a war and a husband who was not supposed to be traveling across borders for visits with his family. In the end, Awo's mother decided that her oldest children deserved a life beyond the rooftop of the apartment in Kenya. She phoned Awo's father and told him that the family would be separated: she and the three oldest would leave for America; Ayan would live with him and his parents; and little Saredo would be sent to Maryam's home village to be cared for by her beloved stepmother. She quieted his protest, reminding him that it was her stepmother who had taken care of her as a child and was fully equipped to do the same with her own child. She reminded him of a simple fact that they both believed deeply: "Life is too valuable to face with fear."

On the day the family was scheduled to leave for America, Awo's mother, with her hair done, her makeup on, her clothes flowing around her slender body, cuddled the baby to her breast. Their flight was scheduled for the evening. The woman spent all day, from sunup until sundown, crooning to the baby girl in her arms, "Saredo, eat, my little one, eat as much breast milk as you can. You will need it in the days ahead."

Just before the family had to leave for the airport, their grandmother quietly approached Awo's mother and took the sleeping child from her arms. Awo's mother went to Ayan, the toddler girl, and held her for a moment, touched her cheek tenderly, before carrying her down the steps of the apartment building. In the street a car waited to take them back to Somalia. Awo and her brothers watched from the rooftop as their mother helped their grandmother and her youngest girls settle into the car. She did not cry. She simply waved.

Awo's mother did not cry later when the family went to the airport. As Awo peered out the round window of the plane during takeoff, she was filled with a sense of excitement and dread. Her mother sat across the aisle, an arm wrapped around sleeping Mohamud, the youngest boy, head leaned back with her eyes closed. She did not cry when they arrived in cold Minnesota or when the landlord opened the door to their small apartment and the stench of dust and old cigarette smoke greeted them.

Later, when it was just the family, the hanging telephone on the wall in the kitchen and a long-distance phone card, Awo's mother told her father, "The trip here was fine. We are fine. The apartment will work. I will take care of these three. You take care of those two."

Her voice was firm, not mad but tight, when she had to remind him that there was no use talking about other possibilities or options. She had pushed for and they had made the best possible choices for the future of their children, the future of the family. She gentled her voice, saying, "One day, when Somalia is peaceful again, we will all return—not as some relic of the worst years of the war, but as responsible adults who have made the most of our lives far away."

Awo's mother did not cry when the people on the streets of Minneapolis gesticulated with their hands and feet at her as if she were stupid and uneducated because she knew little English. She pretended she didn't understand the signals they threw at her or hear the volume of the words thrown at her, or understand their intentions.

Shortly after their arrival, Awo's mother made sure the children were enrolled in the Minneapolis Public Schools. Awo was put in the seventh grade, Mohamed in fifth grade. Mohamud, who had been a middle child, was all of a sudden the youngest child, and he was placed in the lowest grade: third. With the help of other Somali refugees, Awo's mother enrolled in an English as a Second Language class at the International Institute of Minnesota, a brown building across the street from the state fairgrounds in St. Paul.

In six months, Awo's mother was able to take the intermediate English classes. She took advantage of the work-training program in nursing assistance and received her certification. She found a job at a Methodist senior care center on the night shift.

During the day, Awo's mother made her children's favorite foods. The small apartment was filled with the scent of the spices the family knew from home: cumin, cinnamon, cardamom, clove, coriander, and black pepper. She made *kimis* that they ate through the day. In the mornings, they ate them with olive oil and honey or ghee and sugar. During lunch they used them as bread to dip into savory chicken stew and other leftovers from the night before. A couple of times a week, for dinner, Awo's mother made the children's favorite dish, *suugo suqaar*, Somali spaghetti, and they used the *kimis* to mop up the sauce.

Awo's mother became an expert in navigating public transportation. She knew the bus routes and taught her children how to use them. The family took the bus to buy groceries from the Somali stores and the regular American food stores. Together, they sat or stood during rush hour, leaning on one another for stability. Awo's mother proved to her children and herself that she would lead them where they needed to go; even if she was not at the helm, she would be their navigator.

Throughout all of this, Awo never once saw her mother cry.

Throughout Awo's day, answering phones, greeting clients, learning how to track patient records on the computer, she keeps thinking: *I've never seen my mother cry, I've never seen my mother cry. How many people can say this?*

◆

I'm walking through fog.

They are arguing, my mother and father. They don't do this often. This is not a normal occurrence in my life.

She is telling him we have to leave for America, for our education, for the future. She is telling him that no price is too high to pay for our eventual success.

He wants her to stay. He wants his children close. He is comfortable driving the distance—when possible—from Buuhoodle to Laascaanood. There is a future in Somalia. They have parents. Their parents have land and animals. The children can grow up and become good adults like us, still. Their educations have not been interrupted. They will be fine.

She will not hear any of it. Her voice is steel. It can cut. It will cut. It will make such a clean cut through my father's heart that he will not be able to feel it until we are gone.

I'm staring at a wall.

I see my mother and father on this day as characters in a mural. She is wearing black and he is wearing white. There is no setting, no sun, no moon, no other characters, just the two of them on the white wall of my childhood. He is smaller. He is in the background. She looms large. She's beautiful and wise and she stands so tall and elegantly, her head high, facing the blank future, unafraid.

She tells him, "I will come back one day. We will buy land, enough to build five houses. The children will live in those houses. We will be together again in Buuhoodle."

He tells her, "I am a man. I am a husband. I am a father. If you go away, if you take the children, what is left of me?"

She says, "You are a doctor as you were when I met you. Your first duty is to take care of those in front of you. I am a nurse. My duty is to assist your work to the best of my ability."

His exhausted sigh, his defeated sigh, my father, just a man in white, his hands parted, palms open, a gesture always of welcome, of goodwill. He is a warrior fighting the good fight, not with a sword, but with his steadfast obedience to my mother's vision of the world.

The fog grows thick and it grows thin as I grow up and grow older.

◆

Later that day, Awo's mother is preparing dinner for them before she leaves for work. The older woman holds a knife in one hand and a peeled onion in the other. She cuts the onion in half. She sits the two halves on the cutting board, flat side down. Within minutes, there's a pile of cubed onion on the cutting board. The onion fumes make Awo's eyes water. Her mother blinks away the tears. She looks up to see Awo crying and smiles.

Awo is grateful. She is lucky to be so well loved. She waits by her mother's side, much like her father from his place in Somalia. Like her father, Awo will do what her mother wishes in the end. She smiles back at the woman whose image is blurry in the wash of liquid falling from her eyes.

Together, Awo and her brothers go to school every single day they can. When they struggle, they go to the public library, where a retired tutor, an old woman with curly white hair, helps all the Somali children. The tutor is a little plump and wears cream-colored orthopedic shoes. She wears colorful pieces of jewelry, big, heavy-looking bracelets made of painted ceramic, and heavy-heavy-looking necklaces that sit around her thin neck like a collar. At the library, the children not only find help for their schoolwork, but they find entertainment in the books on the shelf or, best of all, with other Somali children.

The children watch television only on Saturdays, between six a.m. and twelve p.m. Awo and her brothers sit together on the one couch in the living area and take turns managing the remote control. None of them fight. No one wants to disturb the fragile system on which their whole lives are hinged—the equilibrium of their mother.

Every Saturday and Sunday, the family goes to the mosque with other Somali people. Awo's mother relaxes with the community around her. She talks. She laughs. She comes up with ideas. When a new family joins the mosque, she leads the charge to go and buy them dishes, fill their fridge, and find them suitable clothes for the seasons. On the weekends, Awo's mother gets to take care of other people, and her children all bask in the attention their mother receives.

Every Saturday, the family gathers around their mother's phone. They use the phone cards to call home. First they call Buuhoodle. Then they call Laascaanood. Every Saturday, in those conversations, they become a full family: a mother, a father, and their children, voices celebrating their gratitude for each other's safety and small successes. Each is reminded of the immense love in their lives, a love that survives unimaginable distance.

◆

Five years after the family got to Minnesota, Awo's mother and father, over their Saturday conversations, completed the required paperwork to bring the little girls, Ayan and Saredo, to America. Awo's father said very softly, "Now, Maryam, I will be alone but you will have all the children with you in America. This brings me joy."

Of all the moments in their lives, it was this one that Awo thought would make her mother cry, but she was wrong. Her mother answered her father, equally soft, "You are a good man and we are doing something good for our family."

On the day the girls arrived, Awo wept. Her mother did not. Waiting before the glass doors to the escalators that led travelers to baggage claim, Awo's mother smiled at every passerby. When the two girls came down the escalator, holding hands, in matching outfits and hijabs, Awo's mother exhaled deeply. She knelt down and simply opened her arms. The girls were shy, unsure of how to respond, particularly Saredo, the baby, the one who had to part with her mother's breasts at such an early age, a baby who grew up having trouble with food, a thin slip of a girl—she waited for their mother to engulf her first in the hug. Awo saw the thin girl's arms hanging like twigs around their mother's neck. Once the hugs were through, Awo's mother looked at the girls with grave eyes and said to them, "I knew this day would come."

◆

Awo sees her mother aging. Her mother is no longer so slender. Her body has softened. Her unshed tears have caused the skin beneath her eyes to grow puffy. Awo knows that her mother's fortitude has helped her children and even their father survive; he lives for the day of their return. From her work at the clinic and her conversations with Somali children and other refugees, Awo knows that people who go through trauma sometimes talk about it. This isn't the case with her mother. Awo's mother never shows her children that there's anything wrong. She never wants her children to worry. She wants to take care of them, to turn a bad situation into a good one, and to do her best to protect them. Now Awo knows that it is her mother's will that has kept their family whole despite the brokenness of the world. Sitting opposite the older woman at the table, her brothers and sisters around her, Awo knows that in the absence of everything, there was always her mother, first and last. She feels the familiar heaviness in her throat and knows tears are close; she cannot bear to imagine a world where her mother won't be, a world where she will have to learn how to navigate not only the road of memory between Buuhoodle and Laascaanood, but the world in between her family.

—AWO AHMED

3

Adjustments to the Plan

IN SYRIA, FATHER had been the coach of the national judo team, a handsome man with eyes the color of green seas. He was not the tallest man, but he had been among the healthiest. He had also been a wealthy man, never having to worry about money. In Damascus, he had a good life, a life he shared with his beautiful wife and lovely children.

I am the third of those children. I look like my father, from the color of my eyes to the shape of my face, to my size. While judo was his work, not mine, it has shaped much of our life together and apart.

◆

Father arranged the three of us younger ones in a straight line. I was the oldest at home, and the tallest, so I stood first. I stood as straight and relaxed as I could. We were home, so my long hair was uncovered, hanging down my back in a loose ponytail. My sister was beside me. Our brother, the youngest, was last.

Father stood before us. It felt like we were facing a fortress. I told myself, *Do not blink; do not overthink this, Bayan. This wall is only a man. He is only your father.*

My mother sat on the sofa. She smiled at me. She was happy

her family was home and together. Her legs were crossed elegantly in front of her. Her slender hands rested neatly on her lap. Her scarf was pale white and it framed her soft face. Her long dress was also white, a fine fabric with delicate designs along its edges. My mother looked like a flower against the dark cloth of the sofa.

The windows were open and the wind carried the scent of fresh jasmine into the room. It had rained in the early morning. The whole city was filled with the scent of the flowering vines and their white blooms.

Father spoke softly, calmly, "Attention."

My brother, sister, and I pulled ourselves together and stood taller to show him we were ready. He shifted, changing from a general into a martial artist. My brother, sister, and I mirrored Father's form: his straight shoulders, his chest pushed out, his loosely bent arms, hands in soft fists held away from his body, his feet planted firmly on the ground.

The right corner of Father's mouth lifted, just a hint of a smile, enough to let us know he was proud.

◆

In our comfortable life on the outskirts of Damascus, in our perfumed apartment, our worries were little. We had a network of extended family and close friends who lived in the surrounding buildings. We walked to school in the early morning and back home again in the afternoon light. At dusk, we sat around our dining table, filled with the simple, good-tasting food Mother prepared with love. After the meal, we took easy strolls in the side streets to greet neighbors and friends as we breathed in the evening air. In our sweet, jasmine-filled city, our family lived like the flowers we loved, healthy and happy in our season of beauty.

We believed we lived in the city with the best weather. It snowed once or twice a year, but the snow never stayed long or caused disruption. Most of our lives were lived in warmth, without humidity or great heat. The first fifteen years of my life were in that city. They were both the best and the worst years of my life.

In judo, resisting a more powerful opponent will result in sure defeat. You must be able to adjust to their moves, leave enough flexibility in your plan of action to respond accordingly at different times. To beat a stronger opponent, the weaker one must learn to adapt, evade, and unbalance to diminish the other's power. This is what we tried to do when the war came to our family.

The war came to us in two days' time. One day we had electricity and running water. The next day these modern conveniences were gone and the schools were closed. We, who had been only partially paying attention to the news, were suddenly the subjects of it.

Restaurants barred their doors. Families shut their windows and drew their curtains. The scent of smoke grew pungent in the place where once jasmine had filled the air.

At first, Mother and Father told us that life would soon return to normal. It was not until the debris of shattered buildings struck our windows that Father moved us to his family's house in a better part of the city, believing that their greater wealth could keep the destruction away. It did not.

In my grandparents' house, we lived with other family

members who had also relocated there for safety. In a way, it felt like a giant sleepover. The young children continued their games. We older ones kept watch over them, listened to the conversation of the adults around us, and then practiced the same talk among each other. We all knew we were caught in a city and a war and needed to attend first to the basic essentials of caring for ourselves and each other to the best of our ability.

One day, I went on an errand. We all knew it wasn't safe, but there was no safety anymore. There was a teenage boy walking beside me on the street. We were not even looking at each other, but we both walked at a similar speed. Two soldiers stopped us. They asked for our identification papers. I took out my bag and found my identification card. The boy beside me did the same. We handed the cards to the plump guard at the same time. Neither of us said a thing. The man looked at our cards, then ran his gaze over us, then focused on our cards again. He handed both cards to the thin guard beside him with great deliberation, his gaze trained on the road before us. The thin one was older. He had a full mustache and eyes that looked concerned. After a few minutes of studying the cards, he handed my card back to me and said, "Go home." I accepted the card with sweaty fingers. I nodded several times to show my gratitude. I walked away on legs that felt as if they were made of melting wax; each step I took, my body loosened. I hoped and prayed to Allah that my body would hold its form and I wouldn't become a squishy mess of a human being. I didn't dare look back. I listened but heard nothing, only silence as I walked farther and farther away. I never found out what became of the teenage boy. I can't know, if I want to be safe.

At home, my heart hammered in my chest, but I didn't

speak of the incident. I didn't want to endanger anyone. My grandparents' house was full of people talking about the everyday details of life, nothing political, nothing dangerous. Instead, Grandmother, Mother, and the aunts prayed every day to Allah. Father and the uncles went in and out of the house all day looking for information and making connections. Like me, none of them came back with anything to say about where they had been or what they had found out. After the incident with the guards, it became clear to me that a return to the life we had known was impossible. Between Mother and Father, there were whispers of a plan to leave.

◆

Practicing judo with us, Father devoted parts of each session to *ukemi*, learning to fall to minimize the risk of injury.

On our living-room floor, in the life before the war, we learned how to fall and slap the floor with our open palms to ease the blow to our backs. I fell over and over, each time responding to Father's observations. Turn a bit to the left or the right. Don't spread your legs or bend them too much. Focus on that slap of your hand to the floor, channel your body's energy there, let it absorb the impact, prepare the earth for your body, prepare your body for the earth. In all the falls, I learned how to trust gravity to do its work. I did not learn how to prepare my body for the impact of the unforgiving ground.

Our family was whisked away from Syria in the dark. The night wind blew in our faces as we huddled close together on a small boat. Rocked by the big waves, we held on to each other for support, a small mass of moving bodies at the mercy of an angry ocean. When we were brave enough, we opened our eyes and shifted our hijabs to see a night sky lit up with stars and a half-moon. Their light swam above us, out of focus and in motion.

On shore in Egypt, our family slept beneath a stranger's roof. Father had arranged everything. The family that welcomed us spoke with Mother and Father of people we'd never met and of those we would never meet again. My sister and brother slept deeply beside me in the room we shared. I kept my eyes open until Mother and Father entered and found their places close to the door. Exhaustion sealed my lids.

Father left us in Egypt. It was part of the plan. None of us knew the particulars of the plan, but we believed, as both Mother and Father did, that this was for our own safety. Mother wept but Father did not.

Father spoke much as he did during our judo sessions, voice even and calm. "I'm leaving for America. I've gotten a visa. From there, I will work and send money back. Once things are in place, I will arrange to bring you all over."

To our questions, he answered in the same manner he administered instructions during the training sessions of our childhood—with firm certainty.

"There's no way we can leave as a family. There are rules about immigration and refugees."

"We can't return to Syria. The family there will wait."

"In six months, no more than a year, we will be reunited in America."

Father left us with a laptop. It was our most precious possession, our lifeline to him and the world. He told us to keep the laptop safe.

On the morning of Father's departure, he embodied the professional persona of his judo training. His hair was combed;

his clothes were in order. His mouth was a line across his face. His eyes were clear and dry. He stood straight and showed us the honor and grace that remained even when the fighting was done and the match lost.

In judo, Father does not practice *shido*, stalling techniques. It is a violation of the rules. He does not believe that a person should prolong a period of nonaggression.

At the stranger's door, Father stood before Mother. He bowed his head low. His curls, thick and black, nearly touched her chin. She put a hand on his shoulder. He looked over her shoulder at us, standing behind them in our usual line. He nodded to acknowledge the parting. He stepped back, then turned. Mother kept the door open for a long moment before she squared her own shoulders and closed the door.

The strangers we lived with in Egypt became our friends throughout the year we were with them. We hadn't expected to be with them for so long but, according to Mother, adjustments had to be made to the plan. In their house, we slept together in the room we had shared that very first night of our arrival. Outside the house, there was talk of revolution brewing and erupting. We heard the media outlets but did not talk among ourselves about the state of the country or the world. It was not safe.

Our hosts were calm and kind, inviting us to take second helpings at mealtimes, offering us clothes and other amenities to make us comfortable. Despite this, in hushed phone conversations, Mother and Father talked of growing risks. One night, after a lengthy phone conversation, Mother informed us that it was time for the family to leave for Turkey. Our friends asked no questions. They said they would miss us, but that they understood that there were more Syrian refugees there and that the Turkish government was more stable. Yes, yes, this wasn't part of the plan, but adjustments had to be made.

Our departure to Turkey, like our departure to Egypt, was done under the cover of night, with people whose names and faces we can no longer remember if we want to keep them safe.

In Turkey, Father arranged for more friends to receive us, take us into their home, and help us find an apartment of our own.

Refugees like us filled the streets of Ankara. All around, men and women spoke Arabic. They said, gratefully, that unlike many other nations, Turkey had taken a humanitarian approach to the Syrian refugees, letting us settle in its urban centers. For the first five months in Turkey, we lived with Father's friend's family and it was like we were visiting neighbors everywhere we went in the bustling city.

Like Damascus, the city of Ankara was an ancient place, an architectural tapestry of past and present, cobbled stone walls beside smooth concrete, spirals rising high beside modern buildings shaped like rectangles and squares. It was more familiar than Egypt had been. It took us away from the monotony of those long days and into more unpredictable, new ones.

With the help of Father's friend, Mother enrolled us in a refugee school. In school, I learned that Istanbul was the only city in the world located on two continents, Asia and Europe, separated by the Bosphorus, the narrowest strait used for international navigation. I found it amazing that the strait could connect the Black Sea and the Sea of Marmara, the Aegean and the Mediterranean, all these bodies of water, that it was a fact. I was starving for facts. In our first six months in Ankara, I learned many facts.

Among these was the fact that in Turkey, without Turkish citizenship and a working man of the house, few landlords were willing to rent out apartments. My brother was barely a teenager. He did not qualify as a man. The landlords refused to rent to Mother, a woman with children who had no source of apparent income. The weight of where we were and where we would go grew heavy in Ankara.

While Father's friend was kind, he could not house us with his family forever. With us, there were eleven people in the small apartment. Mother and Father talked on the telephone for long stretches of time about housing. At the end of each conversation, Mother told him, "Do not worry about us. Allah will find a way."

Mother is a devout Muslim. She believes in her god. She prayed to him. We all followed suit, my brother, sister, and me. We prayed for her prayers to be heard.

They were. We heard news that another friend of Father's had an apartment in Konya, a city south of Ankara in central Turkey. When Mother contacted him, he offered us a room above his family's apartment for a reasonable fee. It was a single bedroom with a bathroom and a landing that we used as a kitchen. We eagerly accepted his offer. We packed our belongings and made the day trip to the big city in the wide valley, with copses of deep green pine trees and low buildings stretching far.

The room was small for the four of us. We stacked our clothes and belongings along one wall. We slept with our heads to the other wall, our feet touching our things. Beyond each other, our only friend was the laptop we shared. The Internet was spotty, but we lived for YouTube, gathered in front of it, counting down the days until we would all be reunited in the place Father had settled, a state called Minnesota.

Father called us each day. His concern for us was growing. Whatever savings my parents had were gone as everything had stretched far longer than planned. We relied entirely on what Father could send. He said he would take whatever jobs were available to him. We pictured him working as he had in Damascus and we were happy.

Our family became closer in our time apart. While we did not talk about the forces at work in our life, we talked often of how much we missed each other and the safe things we could share. We told Father about the weather in Turkey, how hot it was or how cold, but rarely that it was perfect. In turn, Father told us about Minnesota.

Father said that Minnesota was colder than anything we had ever known back home. In response, we assured him we were prepared because Konya was freezing during the winter. Father talked about sheets of snow that formed on the earth for months on end, reaching the ankles, the knees, right up to the buttocks of a grown man. We shivered hearing his words. There were no such sheets of snow in Konya.

In all those conversations, Father never told us about how hard he was working or what he was doing. He sent money on the promised dates so we could pay for our room and the food we ate. We did not tell him about the lack of privacy or how bored we were. We told him that we were together and we were fine and taking care of Mother. We all kept telling each other: there was a plan in place and adjustments had to be made only to ensure our safety, our eventual reunion.

Mother grew sick in our time in Turkey. With the stress of our situation and our living conditions, her legs swelled up and caused her tremendous pain. She hid it from us at first but the pain became unbearable. In the cold mornings, she could barely move her legs. When we asked what was wrong, she refused to talk about it, waving away our questions. She insisted that her faith and her strength would carry her through. I knew she needed medical attention. None of us spoke Turkish, but I was the oldest so I spoke of our concern until she agreed to find help. I became her interpreter, using my body to speak where I had no words, and assistant as we made appointments with different doctors to find out what was wrong. Even more than the war, Mother's sickness made me into an adult. I learned how to navigate Konya's public transportation, its streets, and its medical systems. I was sixteen years old when I became the strongest person I knew how to be. I could feel myself growing older each day.

In the space of those years, it felt to me as if I had lived different lifetimes, but I saw no room in my life for an identity crisis. Instead of being uncertain about myself, I called on everything I had learned from Father's judo lessons, to become more certain in the worlds we were living in. I thought of the different *waza*, the techniques Father cultivated in us. I practiced them in our everyday life.

For Mother's health, I steadied myself using the *katame-waza*, grappling techniques. I coached my sister and brother, and together we comforted her with our love and devotion. We supported her when she needed help but did not offer our assistance in loud words or actions. I made it a point to be where I was needed.

For my education, I practiced the ultimate judo move, the *nage-waza*, the throwing techniques. In Konya, if I wanted to get my high school certifications, I had to do an independent study and pass a test. I knew that my education would be an advantage later in life. So I found the energy inside myself and channeled it into studying whenever I could in that little room we shared—in between doctor's appointments, making dinner, cleaning dishes, and all the other tasks ensuring we stayed alive and healthy.

When I turned eighteen, I was qualified to take the high school exam. There were twenty-eight eligible refugees from the Konya area, and we were to travel to the exam by bus. The trip took four to five hours each way. I had never traveled so far by myself but I knew that a grounded spirit and a willingness to push myself to the edges of what I knew was necessary if I wanted to pass the test. On the bus ride, I began to focus on firmly holding my center of balance. At the test site, I prayed to Allah to help me. I took my seat and proceeded calmly from one problem to the other until the test was done. I learned that I was one of ten students to pass. Passing the high school exam gave me the confidence for a life where the plan must continually be adjusted.

Instead of six months or even a year, it took our family three years to be reunited with Father, in Minnesota. It took him that long to process our paperwork and find sufficient documentation for the family to come as refugees of war. In the end, after all the adjustments, our plan worked—we were together again.

In another apartment, in a faraway city with no scent, we gathered in our line before Father. As the oldest, I stood first. No longer a child. I was a young woman. My sister stood beside me, somehow still bright-eyed and innocent. Our teenage brother was last, now the same height as Father. The fortress of the man we once knew had crumbled. In the years away from us, Father had suffered for us. He'd taken on hard jobs. He was now a worker in a warehouse. He needed surgery to correct the discs in his back, but he couldn't afford it; all the money he earned he'd sent to take care of us in Egypt and Turkey. His eyes were clouded by unshed tears. I told myself: *Bayan, your father is only a man, a man who has done everything he possibly can for his family. He is stronger than he was.*

Our mother, her limbs heavy and hurting, sat on a brown sofa behind our father. Her hands, no longer slender, thick with veins, massaged her knees as she looked at us. Her dress, a coarse fabric that matched the dark scarf that covered her head, framed a face that remained soft despite the hard years. She smiled at me, happy that her family was together again.

My brother, sister, and I mirrored Father's old form: his straight shoulders, his chest pushed out, his loosely bent arms, his hands in soft fists held away from his body, his feet planted firmly on the ground.

The right corner of Father's mouth lifted, just a hint of a smile, enough to let us know he was proud.

—BAYAN TAWAKALNA

4

Up Close, It Is Different

I BOARDED THE PLANE, against the better judgment of my mother and father, for Nyala, the capital of the state of South Darfur in southwest Sudan, not knowing what to expect. I was twenty-three years old at the time. I had just started working for the American Refugee Committee. I was not the team's first choice to go on the trip, but everyone else's visa had been denied. I was a recent college graduate and my résumé was clean. Mine was the only visa approved.

My task was to see what the one hundred thousand people in a refugee camp in South Darfur needed in terms of humanitarian relief. At ARC, we were interested in three primary areas of camp life: water management, health, and nutrition. My family had lived in a war zone; to return to one was the last thing that my parents had wanted for me.

I found myself in the middle of the Sahara Desert, wind and sun and sand bearing down on me. I was thin and six feet tall, so immediately I stood out, a white girl with pale skin, brown eyes, hair pulled back in a ponytail. I saw the people looking at me with wild eyes, bodies tense. The little children who clung to their mothers in the doorways of the camp tents looked upon me with uncertainty. I was swept with a sense of nostalgia so powerful and familiar, I reeled from the unintended blow.

An older man, the cultural leader in the camp, was the first to formally greet me. I held my notebook and pen in my hands and bowed my head respectfully as he addressed me. He held his head high. His eyes were the color of brown glass. His wrinkled lids drooped over the tops of his eyes. His voice was deep and windy and old.

He said, "White girl, let me tell you . . ."

I listened quietly as he told me everything he wanted and needed. When he was done, I looked him in the eyes and said slowly, "I, too, am Muslim. I, like the people in this camp, also come from a history of war and displacement."

The old man listened to my words with grave interest. I could see a dawning understanding grow in his eyes. Then a smile emerged on his face, revealing a set of strong teeth that matched the set of his jaw.

He said, "Yes. Why else would a white girl who was comfortable in one country choose to go to a new country to learn of the discomforts of other people?"

He added, "I understand your empathy and your connections to this place now. Even though we look different, every refugee feels for another."

We became friends. He became the cultural translator for me in the month I stayed in the camp to assess the needs of its most vulnerable families.

I talked to the women who would not look me in the eye, who pulled their garments over exposed arms and legs and sat curled tight into themselves. I asked them things that the men—in positions similar to mine—had never asked: "Why do you feel unsafe at the camp hospital?"

In that first trip and in all the trips that followed, I found in the different countries and people memories of my life in war-torn Bosnia. I found versions of myself, my mother, and my father, and I got to ask them what they needed and to do things that made their lives easier, better, and possible. In every trip I've taken, I've affirmed a promise I made to myself: I want to be the kind of person that I had needed in our time of instability, in the worst years of the war.

◆

I was in the apartment by myself again. It was no longer safe for Mama to take me to my grandparents' several blocks down our street. Since the senseless shelling had begun, there were no more safe places in Zenica. All the mothers agreed: it was better for children to be indoors than out. Although there was nothing for Mama to do at work, if she didn't go to work, we wouldn't get our rations of bread and powdered milk.

The lights in the apartment had been turned off for a long time. The only light we had during the day came from the windows with their curtains pulled close. At night, Mama lit a single candle on the dining table so we could see our way around the apartment and not hurt ourselves crashing into furniture and walls.

I was only four when the war began. For four years, I lived in the war. Those are my memories of my childhood.

In the apartment, Mama kept the candles in a box where I could reach them, but told me, "Don't touch the candles when I'm not home. You will burn down the apartment."

Despite her words, she'd shown me several times how to light a match and put it to the wick of a candle. Each time, she placed a long finger in the air to make sure I understood how serious she was. "Majra, just in case something happens in the night and I can't help you."

I liked the smell when the match lit and the smoke rose into the room.

I loved our apartment. On the sunny days, I wanted to open the curtains, but didn't because Mama said that the curtains were one more layer of protection in the event of any outside explosions. The apartment kept us safe. Its walls were thick. They kept the cold out and the rain away despite the fact that they could not hold the bombs at bay.

Last week, there was a missile strike on our apartment. Mama and I had snuck out to visit our aunt and uncle's house in a small village on the edge of the city, so we were not home. We were all sitting in the aunt and uncle's living room when we heard missiles flying overhead. My uncle, a man with a sense of humor even in the worst of times, looking out the window at the streaks of red flashing toward the city in the dark, said, "This one right here is coming for you guys."

We all laughed.

Later that night when Mama and I hurried back home in the dark, we came to find that the missile had indeed hit our building. The seventh floor apartments were in ruins. Thankfully, our neighbors were safe. The sirens had sounded in time. The grandmother who lived upstairs came down to tell Mama the story of how they all escaped to the basement and to let her know that the families had already moved back into their apartments.

Mama said, "How are the apartments still livable?"

The grandmother said, "We covered up parts of the broken walls with furniture and patched up the roof with tarp."

She said, "It is still safer than being on the streets."

Mama agreed. She offered our apartment if the family wanted to sleep elsewhere for the night but the grandmother said that the families would be all right. When the sirens sounded, we would all end up in the same place: the basement.

After the grandmother left that night, Mama slept with me in her arms, pulling the blanket high up on my shoulders each time it slipped, as if the piece of cloth could protect me. Neither of us slept very deeply.

When Mama left for work in the morning, she laid out my coloring books and crayons on the dining table. She said it was the safest place in the apartment. She wanted me to color and draw and practice my numbers and letters. Mama wanted to register me for school. She had learned from a friend at work that a camp for all the people who'd lost their homes had been set up several blocks from our building and that they had a school on-site.

Whenever we ventured outside, Mama gave me lessons on how to walk on the streets, how to look out for snipers, and how to hide at sudden sounds. Once she registered me for school, I would have to walk there by myself in the mornings and back in the afternoons. I was excited about the possibility of being with people again during the day, especially other children.

We practiced how to walk on the streets when we needed to go get water from a neighboring apartment building that still had a working pump in its basement. Mama and I played a game of hide-and-seek with the snipers who perched in the windows of the high buildings waiting to shoot. We walked, our bodies beside parked cars and the walls of buildings, or quickly inside the bombed-out remains of the houses of old neighbors and friends, never in plain sight. Mama carried the empty gallon containers for the water, two in each hand. I held on to her shirt and moved as if I were a part of her body, like a tail. We always felt like winners when we made it safely to the apartment building with the working pump. The lines were always long, full of other women and children waiting to fill their buckets. On the way home, much slower because the water containers were heavy, Mama jumped each time there was a noise around us, a pop, a rock thrown, a voice from somewhere. My poor heart pounded in my chest cavity so hard that I kept a hand against it the whole way home. Once we returned to the dim apartment, Mama used pages from the coloring books to draw paths for me to take to go to and from school.

Mama taught me how to read and write early. She used different colored crayons to write out the alphabet for me to repeat after and trace. I practiced until I knew the alphabet and then practiced some more until I could read my letters and write simple words. Whenever I grew restless, we played quiet games together. Mama hid little toys around the apartment for me to find. We raced each other, fingers to our mouths, as fast and as quietly around the rooms of our apartment—the bedrooms, the common area, the bathroom—as we could. Sometimes we played a game of *Do you remember?*

"Majra, what do you do when the sirens go off?"

"Get the key from the hook. Lock the door. Go down to

the basement. Wait there until the sirens go off. Stay there until the neighbors leave the basement. Follow them. Return to the apartment. Unlock the door. Put the key back on the hook. Sit, color or draw until you come home."

"Mama, what do you do when you come home?"

"Race up the stairs and call out, 'Majra, Majra, Majra!' on the landing."

We laughed when we played the game but we never laughed when Mama came home in real life. She was always out of breath. I was always out of breath. Our hearts pounded in our chests in each other's arms.

"Majra, do you remember Papa?"

On the day Papa joined the army, the sun was warm and bright in Zenica. Papa came home in his usual fashion. Once the greetings were done, he moved to a chair in front of the television. His long musician's hands clasped and unclasped beneath his chin. He looked into the dark screen of the television, studying his reflection. Mama was in the kitchen. I was at the table with my coloring books.

In a careful voice, Papa called Mama and me to him.

Mama picked me up at the dining table and held me in her lap on a chair by Papa's. Papa cleared his throat before he said, "I have news. Today the Army of the Republic of Bosnia and Herzegovina came to my workplace to do a draft. I was not drafted but our dear friend was. As you know, he is Catholic. As you know, the army is entirely Muslim. As you know, he would not survive the war in the army as a Catholic man."

I turned up my head toward Mama. Her eyes were on Papa's face. She studied him, her brow furrowed.

"What?" she asked.

Papa cleared his throat; his large hands now capped his knees. He leaned toward Mama and me and said, "I could not live with myself if I let my best friend die. I have volunteered to go in his place."

Mama's body became stiff where moments before it had been soft.

She said, "You volunteered to join the army in order to save your dear friend?"

Papa nodded.

She repeated her words, "You volunteered to join the army in order to save your dear friend." Mama shook her head, but she said, "Okay."

That evening we sat at our square table, around the light of a single candle, and ate quietly. We each had a piece of bread. Mama and Papa drank water. I had a glass of powdered milk. Mama and Papa each took only a few bites of bread; then they piled the leftovers on my plate as they did every night.

They both said, "Majra, eat up so you can grow up."

Mama and Papa sat on either side of me, their arms resting on the table.

In the candlelight, Mama looked pretty with her brown hair tied back in a ponytail, her eyes large and shiny, her face thin and smooth. Papa looked very grave, his hands clasping and unclasping on the table. Mama said that when I was born, they were only twenty-three years old. Papa was afraid to hold me. He was scared of being my father, of breaking my small body. It took Papa two whole months before he actually held me for the first time.

I stuffed pieces of bread into my mouth. I allowed my cheeks to grow big with chunks of bread. I opened my eyes very wide. I turned my head from one side of the room to the other very slowly, like a puppet. Both Mama and Papa rewarded me with a laugh. They shook their heads at my game, finished their waters, then got up and walked toward the side of our apartment with the windows facing the street.

Papa opened the window and took out cigarettes from his pocket. He lit one for Mama and then one for himself. They looked toward the gray skies of evening and talked in low voices.

Once I swallowed the bread, I asked from my place at the table, "Why do you smoke so much?"

One of them, I don't remember who, told me that they did it because it helped with the hunger.

After Papa left for the war, it was just the two of us.

Papa visited whenever he could; whenever the army was within traveling distance, he'd come home. On his trips home, he tried to make it fun. He took out his instruments and played songs for us to sing and dance to. He was a musician again. When Papa came home, he used his understanding of how things worked to come up with tricks to make life easier for Mama and me. He was an engineer again. He hooked our television up to a car battery.

One time we saw a BBC clip of a soldier exchange. We realized that one of the soldiers was a beloved relative we all thought was dead. Mama ran to the phone—which worked throughout the war—and called his wife. Papa held me in his arms as we listened to the sound of Mama and the relative crying together on the phone.

Whenever Papa visited, he went out at night to siphon gasoline from abandoned cars on the street, so Mama and I had cooking fuel when he was gone. It wasn't until it was time for him to leave us at the door to our apartment that Papa became a soldier again, his long, thin fingers holding fast to a gun.

◆

I hated when the sirens sounded. When Mama was home, she pulled out an old sled she kept in the closet and placed it in the hallway, outside the apartment door. She grabbed my coloring books and crayons and placed them in my lap on the sled. There were no windows in the hallway.

She always said, "Majra, no matter what, you stay here. You sit, Majra. I'll run and get things ready, you stay put."

Mama ran around the apartment gathering things in case we had to make a quick escape from our building. I sat in the dark hallway, in my sled, with the coloring books as my friends.

When Mama was at work, I had to follow the rules. I grabbed the key. I left the apartment, making sure to lock the door after me. Sometimes, there were thieves who took advantage of the sirens. I walked down the six flights of stairs to the basement. In the basement, I had to find a place to stand beside a wall; I had to be alert so I could kick at the big rats when they came near me. I ignored the cockroaches that climbed the walls and scurried along the floor. When it rained, the basement filled up with dirty water, and my feet and clothes got soaked.

Breathe and wait, kick the rats, stand until the adult neighbors say, "Majra, it is safe now. You can go back to your apartment."

In the apartment, I resume my normal routine.

In the long weeks when we heard no news of Papa, Mama told me things to make me feel better.

If she got an extra slice of bread from a kind neighbor, she said, "Your father dropped it off at the neighbors' when the army passed through the city today."

When Mama presented little gifts, like a hot rod car, she said, "It is a gift from your father and it comes with a letter."

In those moments, I knew it was her way of getting us both to believe that Papa was all right.

◆

Mama had five miscarriages during the war years. She did not have enough food, so the babies inside her died one by one. I was her only child. It was not my parents' choice or mine. But we are all reminded that I was lucky to have been born before the war.

When Mama tells me stories about when I was born, she always begins, "Majra, you were born in the most perfect month of the year. You were born in July, when the weather was perfectly warm in Zenica. In August, it would have been too hot. In June, it would still be cool with the breezes from the mountains. In July, it was perfect."

On the map of Bosnia, Mama showed me our hometown and told me, "Majra, Zenica is the middle of our country. See here?"

She pointed to a little black dot.

"Our city is the pupil of the eye of this nation. Do you know what a pupil is?"

I pointed to my eyes.

"Yes, our city is the pupil of the country, and you, precious one, are the pupil of my eye."

Mama had been a bookkeeper. She had studied economics in school. She was a professional volleyball player before I was born. During the war years, though, everyone called her simply "Majra's mother."

Near the end of the war, something horrible happened. Papa had returned home. We'd just gathered around the dining table when we heard a giant explosion, so loud and close to our building that the walls shook. The building across the street from ours was hit by an unseen missile. Papa ran to the window. Mama ran after him as they yelled for me to stay back. Despite their words, I ran after them. From our window, we all watched as the people on the other side of our street came tumbling out their windows in slow motion and landed on the hard pavement like spattered paint. The side of the building started crumbling. Through the window we heard people's screams of pain and then the cries of an ambulance making its way to help. When Mama and Papa realized that I was watching everything alongside them, they both pulled me close. Their breathing sounded like wind in my ears.

We returned to the table and the unfinished bread on my plate. Papa told us that the worst massacre on European soil since World War II had happened in a village called Srebrenica.

He said, "Thousands of Bosniak men and boys have been killed by the Bosnian Serb army. A friend told me about how his mother had taken all her boys to the town square and told them each to walk in different directions. She knew that certain death was coming for them if they stayed at home. She'd rather they leave her than die with her. In the end, two escaped and three were killed."

Mama reached out her hand to hold his shaking hands on the table.

When the war ended in December 1995, the whole of

Zenica had become a ruin. I was eight years old. Where once we had been an urban center, the biggest steel center of Yugoslavia, we had become a site of crumbled rock and stone. Of the 180,000 people who lived there, there were countless missing, but we knew that we had not suffered more than other people in other places. The only thing that remained unchanged were the facts of our city's geography; we were still in a valley surrounded by snowcapped mountains. In the years after the war, Mama got pregnant again and gave birth to a baby they named Amra. My family applied for resettlement.

In 2001, our family was accepted. We arrived in Minnesota on July 11 of that year.

A Bosnian family who had resettled earlier took our family in. Within a month, they had also taken in two other families. There were eight adults and eight children living in a three-bedroom, one-bathroom house in St. Louis Park.

For my thirteenth birthday, the family took me with them to Sam's Club. I could not believe what was before me: boxes and boxes full of food and supplies. They smiled at my wonder. At home, that night, they presented me with the biggest chocolate muffin I had ever seen in my life. Everyone sang "Happy Birthday" to me. I thought we were all going to share the giant muffin, but the host family laughed and took out a case full of equally big muffins and said that we would each have our own.

I went to Macalester College. I knew exactly what I wanted to study: international studies and economics. I wanted to help rebuild what the wars had broken.

Richard Holbrooke was our freshman convocation speaker. He was the man who had drafted the peace agreement that ended the Bosnian War. As he was talking, I felt the goose bumps rise on my arms, not because of the content of his words, but for the fact that life had brought me to this moment in time.

In my junior year of college, for a moment, I questioned what I wanted to do and who I would become. Then I discovered that I had been placed in Kirk Hall, in Kofi Annan's old room. Kofi Annan was then the seventh secretary-general of the United Nations. I reckoned with myself.

There was always only one thing I would ever become, this child refugee, a person who knew and understood what it was like to grow up in a war. I had to become brave and I had to use whatever means I could find to save the pieces of myself that were in danger of dying in that lonely apartment where I waited for peace.

—Majra Mucić Gibbons

Part II

CERTIFICATE
OF HUMANITY

5

When the Rebels Attacked

WHEN THE BULLETS flew toward our house, some entered through and tore the tapestries at the windows. I had come home early from the guesthouse that day to check on the children and the maid as was my habit. Albert was not yet home. I was holding the baby and talking to the maid. She was telling me we were nearly out of diapers. It was then that the sound of guns rang from outside. I screamed for my children. The lot of them ran toward me from different parts of the house. The maid, a young woman, hands to her ears, sat on the ground and started shaking. The children and I had to pull her along as we crouched low to the ground and made our way into the nearest bedroom. It was the children's room. I whispered for them all to be quiet. We hid in the bedroom, the baby close to my bosom, until the neighborhood around us grew quiet again. I signaled to the maid to take the baby. I crawled to the only window in the room.

The window was open. A cooling wind came through and I realized I was soaked in sweat. I peeked at the world from the corner of the window. I saw that the sun was still shining and the world was as it had been: all the uniform houses sitting in their rows. I could see a few blocks away that the neighborhood store was still open. A bird chirped nearby.

The baby whimpered. I thought, *We only have a few diapers left in the house.*

I got up and signaled for everyone else to follow suit. I pulled at my jacket. I was still in my work clothes.

I said, "I should go and buy some diapers. We'll need them if anything gets worse."

I asked the maid if she was fine taking care of the kids. She said yes. I told my older children to behave and stay indoors.

I paused only a little at the front door. When I opened it, the day spread out wide and far around me. The streets were empty but for a hen and her chicks pecking at the dirt at the right corner of our house. I grabbed some bills from my wallet.

I said, "I'll be back soon."

I walked to my neighbor and dear friend's house. I called out to her as I neared her front door. She answered brightly that she'd be along shortly. I took deep breaths of the dry air waiting for her. At the door, she agreed to accompany me the few blocks to the store. We both said, "Diapers are important."

She asked, "Do you want to go and change out of your clothes?"

I answered, "Do I look shabby?"

She said, "No."

I said, "Then I'm fine in the suit and the heels."

As my friend and I walked by the side of the unpaved road, we talked of how strange the day had become. I fingered the bills I had in the grip of one hand. We noticed a car approaching. We did not expect it to stop, although we moved farther toward the drying grass to make room for the car to pass. A soldier sat in the front of the car, driving. He halted beside me. The windows were already open.

He said to me, "What's in your hand?"

I answered, "A little bit of money to go buy diapers for my baby."

I pointed to the store in the short distance.

The soldier's eyes did not move from my face.

He asked, "What am I?"

I answered, "You are a soldier."

The man in the back of the car, the sergeant, opened his mouth, and said, "Freedom fighter."

I looked from one man to the other, dread dripping down my spine.

The driver said slowly, "I feel like killing you."

I saw that he had a gun by his side, on the seat of the car. I said, "What?"

He repeated himself slowly, "I feel like killing you."

I said, "Why?"

The sergeant in the back answered, "He is a freedom fighter, not a soldier."

I repeated, "He is a freedom fighter."

The driver shook his head in disgust and said, "I still feel like killing you."

My whole body had grown very still. My friend had a hold of my arm and her grip was hard and stiff.

We were so afraid that it did not register that another man in uniform was approaching us until he was right beside me. I recognized him as a friend of my husband's. I turned helplessly toward him. I wanted to say I have babies at home. I wanted to say I have not done anything wrong. But I knew that if I said anything at all, the man in the car would kill me. When the friend spoke, his voice broke through the ringing in my ears.

He said to the driver of the car, "Don't do that."

He added, "Let's take the women to the station and we can talk about it."

The sergeant in the back of the car got out of the car with great deliberation. He closed the car door gently. He stood in front of us and looked at us. I was tall. We were nearly the same height. I did not dare look him in the face. I kept my gaze down but trained on his movements. He breathed heavily. Then snorted and turned away, walking slowly around the car to the other side. He opened the passenger door in front, went in, sat down, heaved a deep sigh, then slammed the door closed. My husband's friend urged us with his hands to get into the back of the car. We had no choice but to oblige. My friend got in first. I got in second. He followed after us. We were all silent. The driver shifted the car into gear and it started moving. My dear friend's hand relaxed on mine only when she noticed that the car was taking us in the direction of the checkpoint into Bong Mining Company.

The gatekeeper, a familiar face, came up to the car as it slowed in front of the station. He took one look and discerned what was going on. He knew they were just picking on us. He told us to get into the station office. It was a small square building with a door and windows, usually left wide open but closed on this day. He opened the door and pushed us in, then closed it again.

We were in a darkened room. The body of our best friend, a local man who was kind and funny and thoughtful, was on the floor. Blood pooled around his body. We could see that some of the blood had coagulated. Upon touch, his body was cold. He could not have been dead a few hours. We held fast to each other. I stood there feeling like my feet were not on solid ground, feeling like I would faint one moment and then throw up the next. My body was hot then cold then hot again. I could hear the men talking outside. The gatekeeper and my husband's friend taking on casual, laughing voices, cajoling like they were telling a silly story. The sergeant and offended driver said very little. I was relieved to hear the sound of car doors slamming. I heard the car engine start and tires begin to roll away. My friend and I started crying.

The door opened and light entered the room. I will never forget the sight of our fallen friend in that sliver of sunlight. His neck was broken. His face sagged in pain, eyes rolled back. We looked into the light of the doorway to see the figure of the gatekeeper there. His face was sweaty. He had a hand to his neck as if he was feeling himself for a fever.

He said in a quiet voice, "You can go."

Outside, we decided to take an alternate road home. We didn't want to be caught by any other cars. We were a mere block away from the station. We'd both just finished drying our tears when a familiar car drove up to us. It was the same car. The driving soldier was the same one. The sergeant in the back was the same one.

The driver said, "Keep walking home."

We didn't know what else to do so we kept on walking as he drove the car very slowly and deliberately beside us. When we got close enough to the house, Albert came running out. My friend and I did not dare run to him. When he made it close enough to us, I thought my legs would give out and I would crumble to the ground at his feet, but I did not. Albert was wary. He didn't come close. He stared instead at the men in the car.

It was the sergeant who spoke.

He said in a very calm voice, "I almost killed your wife."

Albert said, "Why?"

He said, "She can tell you about it."

Then, they drove off.

Inside the house, I held my baby in my arms. I knew there would be no more diapers in our lives.

We had no idea that it was just the beginning. The next day, there was no more work. There was nothing. The Germans and the Italians who owned Bong Mining Company had been evacuated. I called and found out that the same thing had happened at the Firestone Natural Rubber Company.

Albert and I both had family at the Firestone Natural Rubber Company. In fact, we had both been born and raised there in Harbel, a township in the plantation. My father had been a rubber tree tapper. Albert's father had been the man who drove a company truck across the neighborhoods spraying for rodents and other pests. Years before we met, when I was just a child, Albert's father had made friends with me on his routine visits, quizzed me on my ability to speak the Kissi tribal language, and when I had surpassed his expectations had given me money and treats. He'd told me, "One day, you will marry one of my sons." Although Albert and I believe that our eventual meeting and choosing marriage was our decision, who knows what those words had done to shape our destinies. What we did know was that our family there was in as much danger as we were.

Albert and I went to talk to our neighbors and our friends. Many were leaving. There was a small group of people who told us they would stay. They believed that the Germans and the Italians were far stronger than any rebel force. The Europeans would return and our lives would resume. Albert and I talked and decided we would stay and form a close network with the other families. The maid chose to return to her home village to be united with her family. She could not bear the thought of being separated. We respected her decision and wished her well. But we could not leave. We had built a good life for ourselves in Bong Town.

The town was part of the Bong Mining Company, founded by the Germans in 1958, but owned jointly in the 1980s by the Germans and the Italians. The town was only an hour and forty-five minutes by car away from Harbel. It was close enough so that we could visit our families whenever we needed, especially my mother and his father who we were both fond of. In Bong Town, we had found good jobs with the company. I was the supervisor for their guesthouse, managing the daily operations to make sure that the guests were happy and comfortable. Albert got a job in the inventory control for the factory part of the mining operations. We were living the lives our parents had dreamed for us as capable adults.

When the rebels attacked and the soldiers moved in, we found ourselves in lives we could not have prepared for. The townspeople fled overnight. Where once children had played, their voices loud and happy from the primary and secondary schools, now the classrooms were empty and silent. If we wanted, we could have lived in them, but we didn't want that. We were afraid of that much space. We became refugees in our own town. We moved from one series of empty houses to the next over the course of a year.

On the telephone, I heard news that one of my brothers had died. I couldn't go see him or be there when they buried him, but I urged my mother and my sisters to come and live with Albert and me. I told them we would share what we could find to eat and trade for the things that were not to be found. They agreed. My mother could not bear to live in Harbel anymore.

My mother had been a village girl. She'd moved to Harbel when she married my father. His family had lived on the plantation and worked for the Firestone Company for generations as rubber tappers. They made a life in a two-bedroom cottage with no running water or electricity. They were thankful that the house was built from concrete and covered with corrugated aluminum. The outhouse was in back. It was not much but it was the life they had shared. After my father died of a sudden heart attack on his way to carry his morning bathwater from the neighborhood pump, my mother's first reason for being in Harbel was no more. With the death of my brother, there were fewer reasons for her to stay—especially with the fear of rebel forces taking over.

In Bong Town, we all took care of each other to the best of our abilities, but the stress of the continual moves was too much for my mother. She made the decision to return to the village of her youth, to the place of her beginning, convinced that the end was near. She took all but one of my sisters with her. This sister who I had carried on my back when she was a baby and had supported through high school wanted to stay with me. The parting with my mother and sisters was bitter, but I would rather part while we were alive than dead.

A piece of me understood, even then, that this was a war that had to happen because we had lived for far too long without the power to determine our future as a nation. I was afraid and I did not agree with the methods but I knew the civil wars of Liberia were inevitable. We were the first country in Africa to declare our independence as a republic, thus we were the oldest. We'd been "founded" by the Americo-Liberian settlers, freed slaves from the United States and the Caribbean—people dreaming of a place that they could make their own, but they were a population that had gotten used to the idea of taking over what had already been, dominating those who were already there. Before they came, we lived as tribespeople, each tribe governing their own way of life very much like the Native Americans in the United States. When they came, they practiced the worst of what they had learned from the white colonizers. We were at a point in our history where decisions about the fate of our country had to be made. While I will never agree that the indiscriminate killing was justified, Liberia was a nation birthing itself, and the delivery was bloody and disastrous.

Our family moved into the last section of houses that we felt were safe in Bong Town. It was afternoon and my sister and I had just finished making a simple lunch when three teenage rebels entered through the front door with their guns cocked. They were already afraid. Their guns danced in their fingers, slippery with sweat. They stood in a small triangle, one in front and two in back.

The boy standing in front said, "Leave."

I asked, "Can I feed my children first?"

The boy to the left said, "No. You can watch us eat."

I moved away from the pot of stew I'd made. My children crowded behind me. Albert had gone out. When would he return?

I said, "I need to pack."

The front boy said, "Only for your children."

He was no older than my oldest. I nodded and gathered what I could into a bag as the boy soldiers gathered around our pot eating with our spoons. I snuck the family bible and a pen into the bag as my sister held my children, who stood watching as the rebels ate their lunch. I knew we had to leave before they satiated their hunger.

I said, "Come, children. Let's go."

The rebels did not even look at us as we exited the door. I carried the youngest and my sister dragged the other two small ones as we started to run, afraid they would shoot us in the back.

At the edge of Bong Town, I heard a noise and turned around trembling, ready to do what I could to protect my children. It was Albert. He'd heard the rebels coming; he'd hidden in a neighbor's house and then followed us.

Albert took us into the bush. He didn't know where he was headed but he knew that we had to get away and get away fast before the rebels finished their meal and decided to come hunt us down for sport. The bush was thick, the canopy of the trees so dense over the little path that all we could see was a sprinkling of sun. The children were afraid and disoriented.

They kept asking, "Where are we going? Where are we going?"

Albert and I kept answering, "Far from here. Far from here."

We walked for a full day and long into the night before we rested on banana leaves beneath a sky we couldn't see. In the morning, we woke up and walked again, dragging and carrying the children as needed.

By nightfall on the third day, as luck would have it, we stumbled upon a small village in the middle of nowhere. There were about fifty people living in the thick of the green. There was a church, a hut with a wooden cross in front of it. We entered. Inside, there were men protecting their wives and children with sticks, rocks, several guns. They yelled for us to leave. They did not want any trouble with the rebels.

They shouted, "Leave!"

I got on my knees and I started begging them, crying, "We have nowhere to go."

The days had been too long and the sleepless nights too short and I had gone through too much and my children were exhausted and hungry and we needed help.

I begged, "Please, please, help us."

I prayed to a God I had grown up believing in at the plantation school in the Firestone Natural Rubber Company. A God that I believed was good and kind and wise. I prayed for a life that was no more and the possibility of a life after this one where we would be free from war and strife. I prayed for forgiveness for any sins I may have been guilty of, any harsh words or actions I may have committed against another. I prayed for mercy.

Mercy came in the form of a thin man with a face full of wrinkles and a scraggly white beard. He was the oldest man in the group. He stepped from the people and turned to them and said, "I will take them and take responsibility for them."

Under his tutelage, we learned how to live in the bush. He gave us a banana-leaf-roof hut with a makeshift bed. Albert and I let my sister and the children sleep on the bed while we continued sleeping on banana leaves spread over the damp earth. At first, the man shared his harvest with us until we planted a garden of our own and were able to harvest. We scavenged for cassava and wild fruits and vegetables, and we shared what we found with the others. We realized that we had stepped into an existing network of people who'd run into the bush to survive the ambushes and the senseless killing. We discovered that we were a mere three hours away from a nearby rebel city where simple goods could be traded and elementary business conducted. My sister and I walked the journey to the rebel village each week to buy eddoes, a small root vegetable similar to taro, high in protein, and carried them in huge baskets on our heads the three hours back to sell to the remote villages around us in the bush. In this way, we didn't die. The life we were living was unlike anything we'd imagined but we came to believe it was the only way life could be lived anymore.

I had one suit. It had once been a beautiful white color. Now it was the color of the dirt that I sat and slept and lived on. During my periods, my lack of clothing presented issues. I had only two pieces of cloth to use. One for the day and one for the night, and when I was waiting for them to dry, I had to go to the river and to sit in the middle of the water to wait for the cloths to dry on the rocks. In those moments, beneath the bright sunshine, I looked down at myself. I saw that I had been built like my father: I was supposed to be strong and tall. In our time in the bush, I could count my ribs. When my younger children saw my naked chest, they asked, "Where's your breast,

Mama, where's your breast?" All I could do was pull at the nipples still attached to my skin.

Albert and I gave every morsel of food we could find to the children. When they were done with the insides of the fire-roasted cassava, we shared the burnt bits they had not eaten, the fibers that were too hard for them to chew through. We ate quietly, never looking at each other. We wasted away, day by day. I knew it was only a matter of time before one of us grew too weak and sick to continue.

Near the end of our first year, Albert contracted malaria. It was not in his nature to complain but I saw the beads of sweat on his face, the red in his eyes, and I knew something was wrong. I cut down the stalks of young banana trees and split them open and placed the cooling insides against his forehead to no avail. When he grew delirious, when the infection had spread to his brain, he lost the ability to speak and I grew scared. The only thing we had to write on was the family bible and the single pen I had snuck out of the house when the rebels came. I handed both to Albert and I asked him gently to write something for me, anything at all. He saw the desperation in my eyes and took hold of the pen and the bible, opened up its front page, and scribbled a small poem whose words I no longer recall.

I knew that if we did not get Albert to a doctor, those scribbled lines would be his final words to me. I knew that there was a doctor named John, the doctor who worked at the Firestone Natural Rubber Company, who was traveling across rebel cities and towns and through the bush treating the sick. It was ten o'clock at night. I pleaded with the men in the village until three of them agreed to carry Albert in a makeshift hammock and journey with me in search of the doctor. A fourth man said he'd run ahead of us first to find the doctor and lead the doctor our way. I remember thinking: *People are still good, this is still why faith matters.* I knew that whether Albert lived or died, there would be no way I could ever repay these men in this lifetime.

The forest was dark and the night creatures were loud. Wild monkeys cried from the tops of the trees. We heard growls from creatures we couldn't see on either side of the path. We focused on walking as quickly as we could with the weight of Albert between us. My husband made no sound as the men and I helped one another carry him along the narrow dirt path. An hour and a half into our journey, as we were ascending a hill, I saw the dark figure of man who had offered to go get the doctor running our way. Behind him was the good doctor running along with his bag.

The doctor, when he saw our group juggling Albert, joked, "You are all so lucky this evening. What a big deer you have."

I said, "John, it is me, Siah. This is not a deer. It is my husband. John, you have to help us."

The doctor rushed into action at my words. He directed us to a small clearing where we could put Albert down. I put a hand to my husband's forehead to find that he was still burning with fever. John crouched beside me and used his hands to feel Albert's face and upper body. He said he wanted to treat Albert but that the fever was too high and Albert's teeth had locked. I could sense the helplessness from the doctor's form and even in the darkness see the tension in his body as he shook his head and then rose to his feet.

I said, "Wait."

I felt the ground for sticks. I found two. With one hand, I opened Albert's lips. With the other, I jammed the sticks into Albert's mouth. The doctor crouched back down when he saw what I was doing. He proceeded to help me. Once the sticks were through Albert's teeth, the doctor had me hold them in place while he opened his bag and rummaged through. He took out medicine in different canisters. He shook a nearly empty one and out came several tablets. He used the canister top and a small rock to crush the tablets. I held the sticks firmly to keep Albert's teeth apart. The doctor stuffed the crushed medication into Albert's mouth, then looked at me and said, "If the medication works, Albert will be fine, and if it doesn't, then I have done all I have the power to do on this night."

The doctor got up and asked if the man who had led him to us would lead him back to the rebel village so his presence would not be missed. I thanked the good doctor, saying again and again, "God bless you, John. God bless you."

The three men picked up the hammock again with me and we made our way back to our remote village. Albert was as quiet as he had been on our way from the makeshift village. A light drizzle fell. Near the edge of our gathering of huts, one of men carrying the hammock slipped and lost his hold. Albert's body slammed to the ground. I thought it was the end of everything. The tears were rising in my throat and my belly tightened as I gripped my end and watched my husband's body sag to the ground before the man could get on his feet again.

In the dark of everything, I heard Albert say, "Ow."

I could not see his face but I knew he was alive and he would live.

We, the men and I, laughed out loud, in what will always

be the funniest moment of my life, when Albert added with
some surprise, "Something hit me."

It was one or two in the morning. The children waited
for us at the entrance to our hut. When the men and I settled
Albert back onto his sleeping place on the ground, I made a
decision that my family would leave the bush at the first opportunity. I could not do this again. What would happen if one of
the children got sick?

A week later we all entered the rebel city. The people on the
streets were too busy looking out for themselves to pay attention to one more war-ravaged family. We walked around taking
note of how normal life seemed despite what we knew existed
in the bush: the hawkers with their wares on their heads, the
cars on the roads honking their horns, the women with babies
on their backs. By day's end, we found a kind family who
remembered Albert and me from the Firestone Natural Rubber Company and they offered us a place to stay. Their house
was nothing more than a cement shelter, with no electricity or
running water. Still, it was better than anything we'd known in
the bush, so it felt luxurious and safe. We spent many nights
on their hard floor, listening to the sounds of the city bustling
with life. In the evenings, we piled rocks into cans and cut thin
pieces of our clothing to roll into rope. We poured precious
palm oil into the cans. I looked at the faces of my children in
the light of the small flames, their faces thin with hunger, and I
gratefully accepted the food our host family offered.

Not long after we entered the rebel city, a French NGO
called Médecins Sans Frontières came looking for people to work.
They wanted people to conduct surveys asking about nutrition.
I eagerly applied. They accepted me because of my background

of working outside the home in Bong Town. With the NGO team and a few local women, we journeyed from village to village asking questions and doing nutritional surveys. I got food for the family: milk, oil, and rice, and simple medicine. When the NGO left I was so sad and scared, but then the Red Cross came and Albert secured a job with the organization as a food distributor.

Slowly, some semblance of a normal life returned to us. Albert and I were able to register the kids for an American Catholic school. My sister told me that she was going to go to Monrovia to become a businesswoman. Slowly, we began to talk of our year in the bush as the worst year of our lives. We began to say things like, "At least the worst things didn't happen."

—SIAH BORZIE

6

Leaving with No Good-byes

MY STORY BEGINS in a small Karen village in Burma where the chickens peck the ground and the canopies of tall trees provide shelter from the rain. At the beginning of the story, there is a man, a spoiled man, the youngest son of a family of girls, and then there is a woman, a competent, headstrong woman, the oldest of six children. There is no love story but they marry. They become parents, my parents.

In my time with my mother and father, they never talked of love as a feeling between people, a shared affection, attraction, a belief, a bond, a relationship that even death could not sever. They only talked of love in terms of country, a country we did not have as Karen people, one of the seven main ethnic minority groups in Burma.

In a life where love was not a language for each other, my mother and father raised five children. I was their middle child, their most stubborn and independent child, the one who questioned everything, sometimes with, but more often without, words. When my father told me it was time for me to become a monk for a season, as good Buddhist men do for the merit of their parents, I gave him a look. It was a formidable look, with my slanted brows, my eyes dark as black fire. My rebellious heart, like their feelings for us, needed no words to be understood. He knew that I complied with his request only for him and Mother, not for myself.

When my oldest sister drowned in a nameless river, in a nameless place, on a day that I would forget if I could, I experienced death for the first time: to leave with no good-byes. On the day that she died, I saw my mother and father cry until they had no more tears. They cried until they were dry. They cried until the words of love they had not expressed choked them.

I saw what happened after a person died; those who had loved them became less fearful, less careful, more recklessly brave. After my sister died, my mother and father were no longer afraid of the consequences. They moved us away from the Karen village I understood as home into the depths of the borderlands between Burma and Thailand to become resistance fighters. We children, like all people who could die, had to struggle for our lives.

They said, "No one will fight your fights for you."

I knew what my mother and father were fighting for: a Karen state. I learned the history of my people from my mother, a woman with broad bones and eyes just like mine, deep and dark, tempered fire. She had been a teacher and she raised me like a student. She told me about life for the 135 ethnic minorities in Burma before the British came and what happened after. How the British set up a hierarchy in the country and for once the ethnic minorities were seen as potentially powerful. She told me about 1948 when the British left and Burma became independent. She talked of how a military regime had taken over and set out to abolish the cultural centers and the traditional holds of the ethnic minorities. We, she instructed my brothers and sisters and me, were born to take part in one of the longest-running civil wars in modern history. She had given me a Burmese name to ensure my survival should she and my father die and the protection of their arms be taken away: Aung Kyaw Soe, but she made sure I knew it was not my name.

I changed my name after I heard the story. I decided that I did not need the shield of an oppressor to survive. I questioned whether I even needed my mother and father's arms, for they were more interested in the national tasks than the work of letting us be children. I chose for myself a Karen name. I became Kaw Thaw. In our language, *kaw* means "country" and *thaw* means "new." I would be a new country unto myself.

I was barely a man when I left my mother and father for the refugee camps in Thailand. I did not ask for their permission. It was 1994 and I had just graduated from high school, which was unaccredited but organized in the fashion of the old British powers. I did not know where my future would lead. Neither did they. I had a suspicion I might spend my entire life in the jungle, living and dying for a place that could never exist in a country the size of Burma. I left on the grounds of politics and practicality.

In a refugee camp in Mae Sot, a district in western Thailand near the border, close to a village full of Burmese migrants and refugees, I enrolled in a medical training program. There I met the first woman who was not like my mother, and I fell in love with her for all the reasons I loved my mother. This woman stood out to me not because she was the most beautiful woman but because she was the most fun. She was not part of a big history she could not forget. She was just trying to become educated so she could help herself. That singular focus drew me. Her wanting to be independent and live spoke to me. I was far from the adults in my life, so there was no formal marriage. We agreed to a loving union. I was too young and unconcerned with what that might mean beyond having a casual bedmate and a conversational partner. In Mae Sot district, surrounded by the lush jungles, close to a waterfall, I took my first step as a man.

In my union with the woman who decided to dedicate her life to me, we had three children together. Three stateless children, citizens of no country, recognized by no nation. My beautiful baby boys were born with dark black hair, skin the color of the earth. Their maternal grandfather, an old man who, like his daughter, belonged to the world as we knew it, not some imaginary place of freedom, gave my sons the gift of poetry, Karen names calling on their worth. Lao Law Kaw was the first; his name meant that he was worthy of a country. Lao Law Hok Koh was the second; his name meant that he was worthy of the earth. Lao Law Moo was the third; his name meant he was worthy of the universe. I lived like a sun, and they revolved around me like planets, the woman and children of the stratosphere.

I wanted to shine brightly for my growing family. While I had never been a star pupil, I had been mothered by a teacher who had taught me how to learn. There was an opportunity for Karen refugees to leave the camp for Chiang Mai, the second biggest city in Thailand, in a program funded by a rich American named George Soros, a man who wanted to fight the politics of the world through the education of its people. It was an opportunity to learn English, the language in which much of the world functioned. Like before, I did not ask for permission.

I applied. The first time I was rejected, so it didn't matter. The second time, I was accepted, and it would matter, but I did not know it at the time.

Chiang Mai was a life-changing opportunity for me. I took a plane for the first time. I saw the world from the sky. I knew that one did not need wings to fly. My heart hammered in my chest, and when I looked down at the earth, my family had disappeared entirely beneath the forest of green trees, the rise and fall of mountains, the valleys of rice fields. I was enrolled in the intensive college foundation course. In one year, I was able to take my GED on the Internet and graduate from an accredited institution in Maine. In that year, I could not return to visit my family because I was in Thailand illegally. Refugees are not allowed to attend Thai schools. In that year, I met teachers from America, Great Britain, and Canada. The world opened up before me and it offered so much more than anything I had known. In its bigness I did not miss my family and the life I had left behind, which I began to feel was no life at all.

After my graduation, I applied for a full scholarship to go to college through the Soros foundation. I did so without second thought. I applied to Mahidol University and Bangkok University. I was accepted into Bangkok. I could not wait to adventure farther away from the place where my family waited. The four-thousand-dollar scholarship I had been awarded provided for everything: tuition, living expenses, and books.

In the four years of my college education, I lived what I knew then and now as the best time of my life. I explored everything. I grew and grew and believed that I would grow with no end in sight. I lived as if I could die at any moment. I lived desperate for joy. There was no nation I was out to build.

I was only building myself. I flung myself at the expanse of Bangkok.

In that big, hot city, among the asphalt and the concrete, I burned like a fire rich with oxygen. My English raced ahead of me and I ran with it from one street to the next. I gained the respect of the Thai people around me and pushed against the stereotypes international people had of the Karen as simplistic. I liked sophisticated things: the taste of cold soda on my tongue was nothing like the bubbles of champagne slipping down my throat. The bitter greens of old were nothing compared to the sizzling meats available on the street corners and, better yet, in the sit-down restaurants on every stretch of the city. The sweat dripped off my skin like the hands that had held me as a child and the hands of my wife and children.

I graduated with a degree in communication arts. I knew that I would not return to the confines of any camp. I would not leave the streets of joy for the exhausted roads of poverty. I knew I could find a job and lose myself in the city. Soros had not considered the draw of freedom for people who'd never known it; they had tied us tightly into groups and assumed we would return to the people with whom we were identified. Their assumptions were wrong.

I had left my parents. I knew I could leave my children. The woman between them, I saw her in my dreams, standing on the edge of a small waterfall of memories, babies pulled close into skirts, eyes scanning the horizon for me. I saw her there waiting forever. I was equal to the tears that sometimes soaked my pillow at night. I knew that the sun would rise in the morning. The city called out in its many ways. Cars honked horns. Peddlers shouted out their offerings of steamed buns and hot soy milk. Even sirens were a call to song, the song of the forgotten, the song of forgetting.

I found a job as an interpreter, an independent contractor, for the American embassy. I helped facilitate communication for Karenni, Burmese, and Kachin people in their search for resettlement. All of a sudden I was no longer just Karen. I had become part of something larger, engaged in work that was helping people like me work their way into futures where they could grow and sink in roots, not merely be vessels caught in the winds of war. I loved it. I applied for and was accepted to work for the International Organization for Migration where I taught orientation classes to Burmese refugees who had been approved for resettlement in the West—something that I myself was not interested in. I was earning good money. I even assuaged my guilt by sending money back to support my children. Yes, I was a refugee, but I did not have to live like one or die as one.

I met an American woman named Jill. She worked on a team sent to interview refugees for resettlement. Jill was tall and her skin was smooth and pale. Her eyes were large and brown and smart, unclouded by cynicism and unfazed by hardship. They were empathetic and kind. They were so unlike my own. Beyond these things, Jill was well fed, well educated, and well loved. She was comfortable in the world, like a rock at the bottom of the river, feeling the movement from above but steady and strong. Most intriguing, she was interested in me and I found her refreshingly interesting. Jill was drawn to me as I was drawn to her—perhaps because I was everything she was not. We became friends knowing we could be something more. Jill left Thailand after her professional responsibilities were through. We'd only known each other for two months' time.

Over email and on the phone through the spread of four years, Jill and I talked of our days. For the first time in my life, I could laugh with someone about the hard things because the threat of them felt far away. Somehow, with Jill, the world was not a place of struggle. Each day our bond grew stronger and stronger. I was not surprised when the time came and Jill asked, her voice soft and her words slow, weighted by all the reasons why ours was a risky match, if she could petition for me to come to America on a fiancé visa.

I was scared. Jill knew about my children and the woman waiting for me. Jill knew there had been no formal marriage between us. Jill knew about my longing for security and my rebellious heart. And she still wanted to be with me. This time I would not be leaving behind a bad situation, which was my justification for everything I had done. This time I would be leaving good circumstances for a reality where I would have to start anew in the arms of one person who would have more power over me than anyone ever had. I hesitated.

But the thing about life is this: when we are unsure, the Universe isn't.

In October 2010, Jill successfully completed the paperwork. I had been interviewed twice. I was approved to leave for America, to reunite with Jill in Washington, DC.

I had been gone for so long, I knew good-bye was not necessary. Like my sister, I would leave with no good-byes. I would be dead to them. The consequences of my leaving would be ours to bear but we would all survive in the end, perhaps be made better by it.

At Suvarnabhumi Airport, I looked at the giant airplane that was to take me across the world. The chatter of soft Thai voices faded. I remembered the plane ride I'd taken from the Mae Sot district to Chiang Mai, the wonder and the magic of that moment, the feeling that my whole world was going to change for the better. Now there was no feeling like that inside me. My palms were sweaty. I wondered if I would ever find a good job when my only usable skill was English and I was going to a country full of English speakers.

I did not cry as I got on the plane. I trusted Jill too much for that. Jill, whom I had spent four years getting to know, more time via the Internet than I had ever spent with my first love or my children or anyone else—including my mother and father, my brothers and sisters. Jill and I had done nothing but communicate, again and again.

On the flight from Bangkok, Thailand, to Washington, DC, I faced ahead and refused to look behind me at the old man I could hear coughing every few minutes or the old woman with a quivering voice who asked if he was all right, or the lie he told her each time she asked: "I'm just fine."

◆

A car honked. I jumped. The cold blew at me. Somehow in my memories, I had been warm, insulated from the bits of icy snow that flew at my face. The sidewalk was wet and soggy. The snow on either side was dirty. It was late winter in Minnesota. I'd been in the city by myself for a couple of months. I'd come for a job as a case manager for a nonprofit that worked with new refugees, Karen, Karenni, Burmese. Jill would follow, but she wasn't here yet.

I thought of the big building on the corner of University and Lexington Avenues, of my small cubicle and the stream of clients waiting to meet with me. Karen, Karenni, Burmese—we were all somehow more the same here than we were different at home. If there were someone to laugh with, maybe it would be funny. Take a people fighting a war, put them in a new country with more powerful people, and suddenly their fight against each other is no longer as important as their fight to merely survive.

I pushed up the sleeve of my jacket with a gloved hand. I checked my watch, a gift I'd given myself in my Bangkok days, the days of making up for lost opportunities, perhaps a lost childhood. I had fifteen more minutes to walk two blocks.

These days, I thought of my sons often. I wanted to know if they missed me, asked for me, thought of me. Who did they reach for in the night when they woke up from bad dreams? In the daytime, when they saw children run into the arms of waiting fathers, did they think of me? If they did, I could not picture it. I saw them clinging only to their mother and each other. My stateless boys. These days I found myself thinking: *I cannot let the sun set on them in that place where there is no future.*

Jill was pregnant. She'd told me this in DC. It was one of the reasons for the move. I needed a sense of community; Jill knew there were Burmese refugees here. Her family was here. She'd grown up here. She wanted to raise her children close to family.

My eyes had misted at the thought of a baby born to a country and a woman with the power and ability to raise her to become someone important, someone with citizenship. I knew I would have to learn how to be a father. This realization dried my eyes.

As I walked into the big building, from the wintry day into

the heated warmth, I saw myself reflected in one of its large windows. I knew what the world saw when it looked at me: a short man in a fine jacket going to work in a nice building, a man who has traveled far away from the place where his story began. I felt what the world would never see: a child seeking a way into the future and an adult looking for ways to return to the past, willing to forgo everything for the experience of a simple life in a village, chickens pecking at the earth, tall trees with canopies thick enough to keep me dry from the rains.

—KAW THAW

7

In the Valley of Peace

I WAS SURE I was lost beneath that blazing sun, walking between the endless headstones. I was doing my best to follow the figures of my aunt and uncle through the maze that is the world's largest cemetery, Wadi-us-Salaam. I could feel the piercing heat on my scalp despite the scarf over my head. Sweat trickled down the sides of my face and my sunglasses slipped down the bridge of my nose. I felt my own foreignness beneath the hot Iraqi sun. I had been away for too long.

All around me, there were headstones, hundreds, thousands, millions of them. In the blinding heat, they all appeared white in the spread of the cemetery. I looked around me hoping for a glimpse of the buildings of Najaf, the holy city that played host to this place, but in every direction I saw only the endless gravestones. The cemetery is on 1,485.5 precious acres of land. It had cost my aunt and uncle, my father and his brothers in America, nearly five thousand dollars to have Grandfather interred here.

I knew from my family that Grandfather's body was buried in a mausoleum with green tiles to represent that he's a descendant of the Holy Prophet Muhammad. It should have stood out to me, but it did not. The cemetery was fourteen hundred years old. There were layers of bodies, crypts holding on average fifty bodies each, all over this place.

I was in the most holy burial ground in the Muslim Shia world, the site of the burial of the first imam, Ali Bin Abi Talib, the cousin and son-in-law of the Prophet Muhammad. There were an estimated five million bodies buried here. Most Iraqi and many Iranian Shiites have relatives here. During the Iraq War, there were between two hundred and two hundred and fifty bodies buried in this cemetery every day. On our way here, Uncle had told me, "There is good news. Since 2010, the grave diggers say that the numbers have declined to about a one hundred burials per day."

I could hear the Koranic verses coming from around me, coming at me from a distance far across the silence of the ages. As I fumbled through the endless rise of cement, I became one of many who'd walked on these grounds.

I'd left this country behind when I was just three years old. I'd left before Saddam Hussein drained the swamplands of the south to seek and kill insurgents—which was what we were called then, we Shiites who'd taken to the streets to protest the government in power, the regime of Saddam Hussein. My family left in a great hurry after Grandfather was killed in 1991.

After Saddam Hussein's occupation of Kuwait began, the American planes had flown over our southern village of Al Fahood dropping sheets of paper with a message from the then president of the United States of America, George H. W. Bush, encouraging the people of Iraq to stand up to the power of Saddam Hussein. Grandfather, a farmer, picked up the pieces of papers that were caught in the branches of the trees he loved. He had planted the trees when he was just a young man so that his children and grandchildren and generations to come would never hunger for the taste of figs, lemons, palm dates, and the other fruits of our region. Grandfather read the pages that fell into the courtyard of our family home. The sheets of paper said that if we didn't stand up to the regime, we'd see no freedom for our people, the Shia, in a country where we were the majority but did not occupy the seats of power. Grandfather, a handsome man who was only in his mid-fifties, a man with serious, piercing blue eyes, and a sharp aquiline nose, became a leading figure in the streets of our village protesting the Hussein government.

For a brief moment, our village was full of hope that we were part of the people who would bring a greater peace to Iraq. From up north, we heard news that the Kurds had also taken to the streets and were protesting fiercely and proudly the horrendous dictator that had taken over our country. From farther south, we heard that many other Shia villages were also overcome with fervor for a revolution to end the rule of this despotic leader. We felt we were part of a movement to call forth a different dawn.

In our home, Grandfather prepared the family for the revolution. He had five sons and four daughters. My father was his oldest, already married with four children. His youngest was my uncle, more boy than man at thirteen years old. In the evening, after our meals, Grandfather gathered us on a carpet in the courtyard beneath those beloved fruit trees. Grandmother tried to censor him with her eyes. She whispered to him, "Even the walls have ears." But Grandfather was too caught up in what the future could look like for our people, for us. His serious, handsome face was at once philosophical and poetic, his hands, the rings he wore glinting in the light of evening, drew in the air in front of his heart a road to the future.

Al Fahood, our village, sat in between the two great rivers of creation, the Tigris to the east and the Euphrates to the west. We were in the cradle of civilization; my people had lived there for as long as we could recall. Countless generations had farmed the fertile valley. The Euphrates River was hailed as "the soul of the land" and the Tigris River was known as "the bestower of blessings." Grandfather never imagined that we would have to leave, or that he would have to die for this place he loved.

At first, things happened quickly in the direction of our fondest desires. Within two months, we learned that fourteen of the eighteen provinces of Iraq had fallen from Saddam Hussein's rule. In our family home, we celebrated, waiting for the fall of Baghdad, the seat of Saddam's power, Tikrit, his hometown in northern Iraq, and its few surrounding provinces. We ate freshly picked fruit and sang songs of joy around the courtyard.

We celebrated far too soon. Within the span of the next month, many of the anti-Saddam forces were out of weapons. The United States, while calling for an uprising, refused to offer support—fearful of what Iran would do. Without American support, we were left with no recourse. Armed with this knowledge, Hussein and his Ba'ath Party went on an execution spree, killing all who had been interested in overthrowing their government. Grandfather and all of his sons, except for my young uncle, were among the first on the list to be killed in our village.

The men in my family knew they had to flee or we would

all be massacred. My father and my uncles fled to the nearby marshlands to hide with other men whose names were also on the killing lists. Grandfather could not leave with them. He could not leave Grandmother; his teenage son; my mother, his only daughter-in-law; or us, his grandchildren; but most especially an unmarried aunt who was wheelchair bound and would not be able to make the escape without a horse and carriage. Grandfather had a plan to sell all the family valuables and collect his life savings, then arrange for a horse and carriage to help everyone escape to the marshes to meet my father and his other sons. Once we were reunited, we would flee the country together until conditions within were more contained and safer.

The date was March 24, 1991. Grandfather, always an early riser, was up before dawn that morning, eager to put his plans into action. He walked quickly from one room of the house to the next collecting valuables. Grandmother followed closely behind him to help him and to voice her anger toward him. It was his fault. If he had not dreamed of a different future, if he had not risen up in protest, then her sons would be safe at home where they belonged. How come he didn't think of the danger? Who was he to endanger the whole family? Everyone she loved and everything she cherished was at stake. This part of the world was all they'd ever known. If her sons, if even one of them died, she would never forgive him. Grandmother was angry and she demanded a peace of heart Grandfather couldn't offer. All he could do was repeat his plan for a temporary escape, reassure her that he would make arrangements quickly and then be home and attend to the details with the family. Grandfather told Grandmother everything would be fine. He took his gun and the valuables he'd collected from the different rooms and the whole of the family's savings and left the house quickly, closing its wooden door firmly behind him, calling for Grandmother to keep it locked until his return.

Grandfather was killed that very morning in the village square. He was caught by members of the Ba'ath Party. They demanded to know where his sons were. He would not tell them. An argument ensued. They opened fire. They shot him thirty-four times. When it was clear that he was dead, they searched through his clothes and the bags he carried. They took all his money and his gun. They even pulled off the rings he wore on his fingers. They watched as blood pooled around his body and called for the terrified village people to witness the horror. A few made moves to go toward his body, but the men who killed him demanded that no one touch it. They said they wanted his body there in the wide open, beneath the big sky and hot sun, rotting for his crimes against the government. Let all the other insurgents in the village be warned. Let the news of his death carry far.

A kind neighbor brought my family the news of Grandfather's death and of the warnings that had been issued. There was little we could do in the daylight beneath the watch of the Ba'ath men, so we crowded together in our courtyard, surrounded by the mud walls my grandfather had patched countless times with his hands, cowering among the trees in the orchard he'd planted. My young uncle, now the man of the house, and the women around him cried quietly throughout the day. Grandmother was consumed by guilt and regret. Why hadn't she sent him off with the words of love that lived in her heart for him, only him? How could her fear have shaken her faith in the man who she had spent her life building a family with? Grandmother was inconsolable, hands to her mouth with a kerchief soaked with tears.

That night, beneath a moonless sky, my thirteen-year-old uncle and grandmother, along with loving neighbors, snuck into the village square to retrieve Grandfather's fallen body. In the family courtyard, they buried his stiff form, without ceremony or light, beneath his beloved trees. My young uncle was the first and last to hold the shovel, the weight of the heavens pushing on his thin back.

News of Grandfather's death traveled swiftly to my father and uncles in the marshlands. They made arrangements for us. They found a horse and carriage for my aunt, who couldn't walk, and the youngest of the children to leave the village for the marshes. From there, we would rent canoes and boats and make the treacherous journey to Safwan, a small desert town on the border of Kuwait where the US Army had set up a base camp. They sent a messenger with information: the streets were not safe; Saddam Hussein's army had taken over the roads and its planes were surveying all other avenues of escape.

Our one married aunt, whose husband had taken no part in the uprising, helped make the arrangements for the family's departure. At the door of the courtyard, beside the fresh mound of earth where Grandfather had been buried, this aunt promised Grandmother that when it was safe she would retrieve Grandfather's body from our courtyard and have it interred at Wadi-us-Salaam. She told Grandmother that she need not worry anymore over Grandfather, for he would know peace in death regardless of how his life had ended. She assured my mother that she would take care of the house and its belongings and that everything would wait for our safe return when Saddam Hussein and the Ba'ath Party had played out their role in the history of our country.

Our family made the journey to the marshes quietly and without interruption. There, my father and uncles waited for us with rented canoes. We and some thirty thousand other refugee families made it safely to Safwan.

We were the last wave of families to escape Iraq via the marshes. After we left, Saddam Hussein ordered the marshlands to be drained. His followers diverted the flow of the mighty Tigris and the Euphrates rivers, destroying an ecosystem that had fed 450,000 thousand people and countless animals and plant life. They dislocated the Marsh Arabs who had lived nearby for centuries, whose whole lives were lived in rhythm with and dependent on what the wetlands could provide. The insurgents that were still hiding in the marshes found themselves easy prey for the soldiers who came to hunt them down.

In Safwan, we all became refugees of war. Each family was given a tent, food, and clothes.

Shortly after our arrival, the American army withdrew from the war officially. We, the whole of Iraq, had been reduced to the fire bombs that flashed across the television screens of America. The death toll of Americans in the Gulf War was 219; 212 were men and 7 were women. Of that number, 154 had been killed in battle, 65 had died from nonbattle causes, and 35 from friendly fire. The Pentagon has never offered an estimate on the Iraqi casualties in the war and has been quick to disavow the numbers. The only official American statement that has been made about the Iraqi deaths was by General Norman Schwarzkopf, who said near the end of Operation Desert Storm, "There was a very, very large number of dead in the forward units, a very, very large number of dead." When prodded by members of the press for an exact toll, he said, "The people who will know best, unfortunately, are the families that won't see their loved ones come home."

We are one of those families, the lucky ones who escaped. But even we do not know how many Iraqis died; all we know is that Grandfather was one of the men lost to that war. But we were not dead yet, and unlike the American soldiers who would all be returning home, we had nowhere to go, no way to withdraw. Under the auspices of the United Nations and with the support of Saudi Arabia and the sympathies of the United States, a camp was built for us in the desert on the borders of Iraq and Saudi Arabia.

I was a child, not yet four years old, but I remember getting loaded onto the US warplanes. I was so afraid, so little, and so unsure, and I clung to my mother, who held tightly to all four of us children, as the plane lifted off the ground, and rose higher and higher into the sky. It was dark inside the cavern of the plane and the American soldiers in charge of us were all men of war who behaved the part, their faces serious and solemn. Beside them, the men in my family, my father and uncles, in their traditional clothes, looked defenseless and unsure about where we were going or what was to become of us. I felt we had been swallowed up in the belly of a flying beast.

We were flown to a nearby town. There, we were directed to board buses that took us to the Rafha refugee camp, one of the six camps scattered throughout the northeast of the Saudi kingdom for Iraqi refugees. At Rafha, we became one of the 150,000 forgotten refugees in Saudi Arabia after the Gulf War. The Americans and United Nations left; we were abandoned in the sole custody of the Saudi guards. Except for early on in the crisis when a few reporters were given limited access to the Rafha refugee camp, no human rights organizations or foreign reporters were allowed into any of the camps. We were not allowed out. There, we lived for five years heavily guarded by Saudi military personnel, with little access to the outside world.

I grew up in the camp. After a year of living in the tent with my big family—Grandmother, Father, Mother, my three unmarried aunts, my four unmarried uncles, and my three siblings and I—we were all moved into a mud house. One of my older uncles got married in the camp and his young family made the decision to leave the camp. He registered for resettlement in the United States. The adults were sad and they cried a lot, but my father, being the oldest, held on tightly to the hope of a return to Iraq, to raise his children and become an old man in our family home among the fruit trees his father had planted. Soon after Uncle and his family left, the resettlement process was closed for all of us in the camp.

I remember the camp like a city. There were thirty thousand of us living in close proximity. The organizers of the camp divided us into small neighborhoods of families and tribes. I went to first and second grade in the camp. I had school uniforms. I had friends who played with me outside our mud house. It was a strangely happy time despite the fact that we lived behind a barricade of wires and men with guns, despite the fact that the young, unmarried men had all been taken into a separate camp away from us. My father, grandmother, and mother whispered of sexual abuse and beatings by the Saudi guards, but in our mud home, we played with the toys our grandmother made for us, traditional Iraqi dolls made out of sticks and bits of fabric. And like any other city in the world, the camp was divided into family groups of those who had more money and others who had less.

My family did not have much money. We were not very popular and lived modestly on the family stipend of eighty dollars a month, using the money to buy things like toothpaste, toothbrushes, and soap. We saved parts of our food rations—flour, sugar, and rice—for our family back home in Iraq who we knew were starving because of the harsh sanctions—believing a return could happen as quickly as our departure. The wealthier families opened up shops and bakeries, restaurants and other businesses in the camp. My family did not frequent these places because we were poor.

In 1995, the United Nations High Commissioner for Refugees came back to the camp to do another round of resettlement. By then, my father had lost all hope of returning home. My young uncle, who'd been responsible for the ghastly task of burying his father, had turned seventeen. He'd taught himself how to speak English fluently and competently. He was hired as an interpreter for the international agency.

The people he worked with were impressed with his intelligence and the source of his fire, which he did not hide: the murder of his father. They encouraged him to apply for resettlement. He began teaching my siblings and me the alphabet after school. He convinced Grandmother and my father and mother that our only chances of knowing anything beyond our homelessness was to leave the camp. He applied for resettlement for all of us. We were unsurprised when we were interviewed—so confident were we in our young uncle—but we were grateful when we cleared security.

My family was taken to Riyadh, the capital city of Saudi Arabia, for our medical exams. I fell in love with the feeling of freedom, life beyond a fence. In Riyadh, I saw cars and I saw lights and we got to sleep in a hotel the night before our trip to the hospital for our exams. It was amazing and I started thinking America would be, too. I was sad to return to camp to await news of our examination results.

We passed our medical exams. We were approved for resettlement. We were given a few choices of where to resettle in the United States. We chose San Diego, where my uncle who had left in 1992 had gone, our young uncle leading the way.

On May 22, 1996, my whole family arrived in San Diego, California. I was eight years old. I didn't know what to expect of the world beyond my one night in Riyadh. I was astounded by the ocean and the mountains. I had no idea that with little money and no language skills, our family was not equipped to live in such an expensive city with few job opportunities, but it did not take any of us long to figure this out.

For we children, English was not too hard. By the end of our first year in school, we were speaking English well. This was not the case for my father, mother, or grandmother. The low-skilled jobs were all taken. After some thought and research, two of my uncles decided that we should move to Minnesota, a state with many low-level jobs. More enticingly, they wanted to open a small grocery store so that we could work for ourselves and build something in America. My father thought that the idea was good enough, so our time in California did not last long.

My father and one of his friends took turns driving us across the country in a used van. We all kept our gazes glued to the window. America was a movie with never-ending highways, cars and trucks full of people going places. We could have kept the movie going forever, but eventually we got to Minnesota and became one of seven Iraqi families in the state.

In Minnesota, my young uncle quickly distinguished himself academically. He was accepted into St. Cloud State University where he received his bachelor's and master's degrees in teaching English-language learners. After his graduations, he found teaching positions for himself all over the world. When he returned from his international study of education, he applied to the University of Chicago. There, he used the fire in his belly to work on a doctorate specializing in refugee children and education. He wanted to speak to the traumas of war in the classroom, to use his own personal experiences to fuel the work of making education successful for children who had learned of death before they could meet life fully.

My own journey as a student has not been as smooth as my brilliant uncle's. Before September 11, 2001, school was fine enough, but after that day everything changed for us in Minnesota. My family was living in Fridley, a close suburb of Minneapolis. I was in eighth grade in a predominantly white school. The first incident happened in art class. A group of kids started saying that I was Osama bin Laden's sister. When I told them I didn't know who he was, they started asking if I was bald underneath my scarf. I had never heard of Osama bin Laden before that day but I knew they hated him because they all started to hate me. I made what I thought was a brave decision; I told the principal of the school about the incident. The principal talked to the students who had said the mean things to me. I thought that the principal's conversation with the students would make it easier for my sisters and me, but the principal didn't talk to the teachers, just the students, and that was only part of the problem.

I had a social studies teacher whom I'd known since seventh grade. He had been kind to me. After the fall of the twin towers in New York City, he changed. He started being hostile. He couldn't look at me in the classroom. I started to hate being there. I knew he didn't want to see me, and I didn't want to see him anymore either. I struggled to get to the end of the school year.

My sisters and I could not tolerate the thought of returning to school in the fall. We pleaded with our mother and father to be homeschooled. They saw our fear and the meanness we were encountering at school; as a family we made the decision to enroll us in an online public high school based in Chicago. We received textbooks in the mail. We studied by ourselves at the dining table. We took tests on the computer. We passed the tests that were graded by teachers whom we never had to look at and who didn't have to avert their gazes from ours. We advanced from one grade to the next without meeting anyone outside of our house.

Our mother and father, the whole of our small but growing community, faced a backlash from the Minnesotans around us who believed that our being Muslim equated to us being terrorists. In 2003, because there was no more chance of a return to Iraq and because of the pressures of living in America without citizenship, my mother and father made the decision to become citizens. My brothers and sisters and I were not yet eighteen, so we all got our citizenship with them. We went to the swearing-in ceremony just days before Saddam Hussein's government collapsed.

It was early spring. The snow had melted off the ground because of the rains. Green grass was surfacing among the yellow neighboring lawns. The spring skies were blue and filled with warm sunlight. The early dandelions were growing fiercely along the cracks in the concrete though not yet blooming. The small-flowered crocus with its light petals of soft purple stood up in patches that made people happy winter was over. That morning, I got up like usual and prepared for a regular day, but when I went into the family room I found that everyone was standing or sitting, staring at the television. They were watching a news network and a blond woman with a strong voice said, "Saddam Hussein's government has been toppled. The phone lines all over the country have been cut."

We looked at each other. Was our family there alive? My mother's whole family was there. Her father had died a long time ago but her elderly mother, one brother, and three sisters were all still in Al Fahood. Were they safe? My aunt who had been married, who had helped us escape after Grandfather was killed, and afterward had found a way to reach us in America, who had made sure that Grandfather's body had received a proper burial and secured a plot for him at the most sought after of the Shia cemeteries, Wadi-us-Salaam, was she still alive? The day we'd all been waiting for had come and all we felt was worry about the people we'd left behind. The sunshine and warmth we'd been waiting for all winter, all those crocuses to be found among the grass, could not lure us away from the television that day and in the days to come.

On April 9, 2003, my family and I huddled around our television as we watched the statue of Saddam fall. My mother, telephone to her ear, called and called a line of numbers she'd written in a notebook, until she was able to get hold of a neighbor of the family's and was assured that everyone we loved had survived. Then we celebrated. We had finally won. The uprising that had killed Grandfather had not been for naught. We would one day be able to return to the orchard Grandfather had planted after all, and we children would finally taste the mythical fruits from its trees.

For my youngest uncle, the return was much closer than any of us had imagined. He secretly bought himself a plane ticket in June 2003. Al Qaeda had entered the country. All the news outlets were talking about terrorism and extremists. The country was not safe. We all thought that my uncle was working hard at school in Chicago. None of us knew what he'd planned and what he'd done. That summer, my young uncle returned to Minnesota to visit us. He sat his mother down before the television. He played a video for her. In the video, we saw our family in Iraq sitting together, talking. We saw our very own uncle, sitting in that very same living room, eating food, having a reunion with family members from Iraq. Grandmother could not believe her eyes, looking from him to the screen as if he were a ghostly apparition of her son, not made of flesh and blood.

My young uncle told her softly, "Mother, you can safely return now."

That winter, Grandmother and my father returned. They visited Grandfather's final resting place. They came back saying that the family home had stood waiting empty in Al Fahood for us all.

That next year, my sisters and I made the decision to return to Fridley High School. We had seen history correct itself. We wanted to show the students who had made us afraid that we were brave like the Iraqi people who'd overthrown Saddam. We entered the familiar doors of Fridley High School with our heads high, one behind the other. We all worked hard, and I was the oldest, so I graduated first. I enrolled at North Hennepin Community College. In college, I was surrounded by other refugees from around the world, from all these wars I had not known, all these places I could not have imagined. For a final project, I chose to do a presentation titled "Life in a Refugee Camp." It was the first time I could tell my story. Standing before twenty students, I stopped being embarrassed. The faces of my classmates showed me that they were interested and engaged. The professor gave me an A.

That A has given me the courage to live in my story fully and fearlessly, to say to anyone who wants to judge me or any other refugee in the world, "Judge me, judge us, only after you have heard our stories."

My own return to Iraq did not happen until 2009. I had become a woman—not just any woman, but a woman who had married a Saudi Arabian, a people my family had feared in the refugee camps, a man who was able to show them and me that we shouldn't be afraid of each other anymore.

Together, my husband and I returned to a part of the world I knew only via news outlets and the stories from my family. In

Saudi Arabia, I fell in love with Riyadh all over again, my first free city, the city of lights, that first hotel I slept in on that far-away night. Ensconced in his family, my new family, I discovered the beauty of the country that had hosted us refugees from across its borders. I saw clearly the limits of my experiences as a refugee child in Saudi Arabia.

I was eager to return to Iraq. When we did, I discovered a country that was chaotic and poor. Its streets were filled with trash. The remnants of the wars of the last quarter of a century were everywhere, from the buildings still shattered from the missile strikes that had hit into the beating hearts of the cities, to the broken bridges that once crossed rivers flowing with life, now full of debris, to the men and women on the streets who looked upon me as foreigner, to the children who laughed and raced down hard-baked roads with their dark eyes full of curiosity and the fire of loss I see in my young uncle. Nothing was as I had imagined or hoped for.

I discovered that while the family home was standing, Grandfather's beloved orchard was long gone. There had been no one to tend to the trees in all the fighting and the haunted years that followed. They'd grown old, and diseased, and died. The house had no electricity. There was no running water. It was uninhabitable. Our fields were empty. During my time in Iraq, I was filled with a sadness for my country and my people, a feeling of my own short-lived story, our tragic history.

I visited Grandfather's grave in the hopes of meeting, if only in memories, something of the man he had been, the handsome young suitor, the farmer and the fearless revolutionary, the dreamer and the man whose death ended so many of our dreams.

As I journeyed, blinded by the unforgiving sun, toward his final resting place, I saw all around me in Wadi-us-Salaam, Arabic for "Valley of Peace," tokens of war and the layering of history. I saw the statues that we've built for those we loved, memorials for men and women who had lived and died. I was overcome by the knowledge, with each step over a gravestone or as I caught my breath beside one, of how valuable our lives are. I realized how each person who had died and been buried in this cemetery had lived loving and protecting the essence of who we are as the Shia people so that I and my children of tomorrow can live.

—HAWRA ALNABI

8

Certificate of Humanity

I WAS AN OBEDIENT son who wanted to follow my heart, so I defied my mother and my father and returned to our beloved Kandahar.

◆

Kandahar of my heart, of my country, of my blood, and my skin. Kandahar, with her dry sand and her stretches of desert along the edge of the Arghandab River. Kandahar, known throughout Afghanistan for its pomegranates and its grapes, known by others for its marijuana and hashish. Kandahar, the land of my birth, the birthplace of my ancestors.

◆

I was nineteen years old. I had just finished a degree in business administration at Iqra University in Quetta, in Pakistan, and was working on a nonprofit initiative to help people start businesses in local economies, to model how men and women could work together effectively in the Muslim world. The war on the other side of the border was still going on, but there were humane organizations trying to help the war-stricken people. I applied to work as a bookkeeper for the United States Agency for International Development believing that I could do some good for my people.

I'd left Kandahar in the arms of my mother when I was just a few months old. I was born on November 30, 1988. It was in early 1989 when the Russians were defeated. The warlords, funded by the United States of America on one side and the Russians on the other, came to Kandahar to wage their battles. One of my uncles was killed in a skirmish. In fear, my family and millions of others left our villages and our cities behind in the hopes of finding refuge.

We found our way to a refugee camp on the border with Pakistan. We lived there for several years hoping for peace in our country so that we could return, but one war shifted into another. When the twin towers went down and a war against terrorism was declared, when Osama bin Laden, who was not Afghani, set up the Taliban in my hometown, my mother and father grew despondent that we would ever be able to return. They applied for permission to leave the refugee camp and move to the nearby city of Quetta in Pakistan. There, they raised us.

Quetta is a beautiful town in the mountains, and for nineteen years it was all I knew, but it was never my home. I watched CNN and BBC on television and I learned English and the politics of a bigger world. In the community, I listened to the elders talk and the young men ponder; I knew of the politics of my people. We all knew that it was US dollars funding Pakistani training that resulted in Afghan bloodletting. I heard the stories from my elders about the homeland. I dreamed of the hot desert sun on my skin, yearned for the scent of the sand, and the feeling of belonging. All around us, despite the millions of Afghans in Quetta, people could see from the food we ate, the way we lived, the clothes we wore that we were not Pakistani.

◆

I returned to Kandahar with the initial protection of USAID. After a year, I was able to call my mother and my father and my younger siblings home—despite the bombs that continued to fall and the suicide bombings that we were reading about in the newspapers. It was not long after their return to our family home that the conditions in Afghanistan forced me out.

At first I received letters from the Taliban. The notes were threatening: we know who you are and what you're doing for the Americans, and if you don't stop, bad things will happen. When the notes did not get a response from me, I started receiving phone calls. They came throughout the day, early in the morning, late in the afternoon, during family meals in the evenings. I could be standing at the local grocery waiting to pay. My phone would ring. I would pick up. A man—each time a different man, but always it was a man's voice—would say to me in Pashto or Dari, "You're wearing a black shalwar right now. You're standing at your grocer's waiting to pay. If you don't stop your activities with the Americans, I will hurt you or your parents, or maybe your sisters, or that little brother of yours."

Sometimes I just listened, and other times I tried to deny the charges. I'd lie and say, "No, no, no. You're mistaking me for someone else. I'm just the son of a small merchant." One or two laughed. The others got angry and talked to me of their witnesses and the documents they had showing my daily schedule, the people I went to see, the places I visited. Each day I grew more afraid, more distrustful of those around me, until the time came when I believed that staying in Kandahar would kill me and my family.

◆

I went first to my supervisor at USAID, an American woman for whom I had a lot of respect. She listened to my story with her head down, her hands in front of her, clasped on her desk. It was a familiar story to her. She'd worked with enough Afghans who had been threatened by the Taliban, and knew of the disappearances and deaths. She told me about the Special Immigrant Visa (SIV) offered through the State Department and told me to apply. She said that as a bookkeeper for USAID I would qualify. However, the government only issued up to fifty such visas each year for both Iraqis and Afghans who had worked with the US Armed Forces or under Chief of Mission authority. She spoke with some reservation, because there was a three-year wait period for security screening and clearance. Neither of us spoke the question in the room: Could I wait for three years?

At home, my mother and father and I decided that the only way I could survive was if I hid in the house and stopped going out. I sent a message to my workplace to tell them I would not be coming in anymore. I sat deep in the bowels of our house, surrounded by the mud walls of my ancestors, knowing that if the Taliban wanted to find me they could simply march through our front door and unleash their bullets. If they wanted, they could drop a bomb on all of us. I couldn't sleep or eat, despite the people I loved gathered around me, despite my mother and father assuring me of their love for me. They

told me that hiding in our house was not an act of coward-
ice but the actions of a reasonable human being. I felt young
under their protection, and yet I was too old and had seen too
much to believe that their love could protect me. Every minute
that I was home that month, I felt keenly that everyone I loved
was in danger because of my living presence.

I made the decision to leave Afghanistan. I made arrangements with a human trafficker and was able to pay the price he
demanded for taking me out of the country: $25,000. I tried
to find a reputable trafficker, one who brought a contract for us
to sign. The first line of the contract was a waiver: the trafficker
was not responsible for my life or death; they had no responsibility to return my body—alive or dead; everything that happened to me on the road to probable survival depended on my
following all their instructions. Even then, they could not guar-
antee that I would make it out of Afghanistan. Other clauses
in the contract said things like, they would divulge information
only when it was necessary and the less I knew, the safer I would
be. I signed the contract with a black pen. My mother and my
father hovered behind me. The trafficker averted his gaze sym-
pathetically.

◆

On a bright day that I saw only through the filtered doorway
of my home, a middle-aged man arrived at our house.

He said, "Your son has fifteen minutes before we go."

He brought me a change of clothes: a pair of blue jeans,
walking shoes, and a T-shirt. He said to take nothing. I
changed out of my shalwar as fast as I could. I wanted every
last minute to be with my family. They all cried. It was not

until we were in the car, on our way to the airport, that I could let my own tears fall. Outside the car window, I saw the broken walls of my city. I saw the war-stricken poverty of my people. I felt our fear.

◆

At the airport, the man handed me a plane ticket and three passports and a backpack with nothing inside other than a second pair of walking shoes. The first passport was a green Pakistani one. The second was a maroon Spanish passport. The third was blue, my own Afghani passport. He told me I would be flying to Dubai. He pointed to two men, already through security, standing together.

Once I cleared security, I joined the two men. We each wore a backpack, a pair of jeans, and a T-shirt. We talked in whispers. We had each paid $25,000 to leave Afghanistan. We had all worked for one American agency or another. I was the youngest and the only one unmarried. One man's wife was pregnant. The other had three young daughters, ages two to four. We would be traveling together.

◆

We made it out of Afghanistan without any problem. It was at the airport in Dubai that my bag containing the three passports alerted the officials. The two other men had cleared security. I was the third in line. I could see the image of my bag's contents on a screen. There were the walking shoes. Then there were the three passports. The man behind the screen talked to his coworker. They motioned for me to leave the line. In a separate alcove, an elderly man with fierce eyebrows and dark, penetrating eyes, said, "Open your bag." I nodded because I could not speak. My throat was tight. My arms were tight. I unzipped the bag stiffly. Inside, my hands reached for the passports and fumbled around. To my surprise, I felt that the bag had a false bottom. I tucked the passports inside as quickly as I could. I pulled out the shoes like they were heavy and held them up to the man. I gestured for him to look inside my empty bag.

He shrugged his round shoulders and waved me off. That was it. As I walked away, I reminded myself to unclench the muscles in my arms and my back. My fellow travelers had waited for me at a nearby column. We exchanged glances but no one said a thing.

People walked around us in the bright airport. It was a big shiny place. The ceilings were high. The escalators had lights along the rails that were blue and white. The second floor had colorful wall panels. Merchants sold goods in beautiful stores along the walkways. It was clear that we were in a country of prosperity and peace. People talked among themselves casually. There was no mood of panic, no smell of hot sweat in the air-conditioned terminal.

We didn't have to wait long. A Pakistani man approached us and said we should follow him. He was a connection. Outside, the heat was sweltering. He took us to a car. He drove us into the heart of Dubai. Buildings, like spacecrafts, rose up from the earth toward the high skies. Surrounded by blue water, the place smelled of money. Palm trees waved from the sidewalks, but none of us was in the mood to wave back. We were shocked. We had gotten used to war. So much wealth, so much peace was blinding and deafening, and it was a relief when the man checked us into a hotel. In our room, he gave us the things we needed: toiletries, changes of clothes, and said, "I will come by and pick you up for meals."

◆

In that hotel room, equipped with three beds, we waited for five or six weeks. At first we stayed only in the room until the man came to pick us up for meals. Then we got a little braver and started to walk around the area outside our hotel. Our pockets were empty so we could not buy anything, but we looked at price tags and saw that everything was expensive. We'd return from our excursions and pray, asking for patience, for strength in our hearts, for the lives of the people back home in our country. Each time, we ended prayers with a call for peace.

I knew then that leaving my country was not a solution to the problem of war. In Kandahar I had left not just my family but my heart. How can a man make his way in the world when his heart is tethered to a place he may never see again?

Somewhere in that long wait, one of the men told us he was leaving, that he had to return home. He could not wait with us anymore. There were people waiting for him. The two of us tried to stop him. I said, "We're only at the beginning of this journey. If you leave now, you'll destroy our morale. Please stay." The other man said, "You have to believe, you can't go." His answer was, "I cannot stay." Short of holding him back physically, which we would not do to our friend, we watched him leave the hotel, knowing he'd broken the contract we signed.

Soon after he went, our connection brought in another Afghan man who had worked for the United States.

Every day, we asked the connection when we would leave.

Every day, he said, "Tonight."

Every night, we waited for him, teeth brushed, shoes on.

Every night, he kept us waiting.

We began to think that we'd never leave. We stopped trusting the connection, so we stopped gearing up to leave. Then one night, there was a knock on the door. I woke up to open it.

The connection came into the room with urgency.

"We're leaving," he said. "Bring nothing but your backpacks."

It was midnight. We clamored into the bathroom to brush our teeth. We put on our shoes and grabbed our bags and followed the man outside. It was a hot night. I imagine that the night was full of stars. It was November or December. My birthday had come and gone. I was now twenty-four. I thought of that on the drive to the airport.

At the airport, the connection handed us tickets to Serbia. He told us that we would leave using our Pakistani passports.

◆

We got on a plane headed for Serbia, bringing us closer and closer to the free world, farther and farther from home. I had expected to arrive at another big, shiny airport, but to my surprise the airport in Belgrade was small. Our plane landed quite late. After we deplaned, most people left, met by family and friends. We, the three of us, found a row of seats outside the gate and sat down in a general area. It was not long before we drew the attention of the people behind the walls of the airport, the police officers monitoring the cameras. We were surrounded by police, equipped with guns. They spoke in English, asking us who we were and what we were doing in the country. We said nothing, pretending not to understand them. As they tried to talk to us, we took turns going to the bathroom. In the closed stall, I hid the Pakistani and Afghani passports in my underwear and took out my Spanish passport, just in case. After some long minutes of us raising our hands to our sides and looking at each other with confusion, they left us alone to calm our fears.

The gentle light in Belgrade entered the waiting area slowly as morning dawned and men and women arrived in uniforms to stand behind kiosks and passengers began streaming in. We were exhausted from our long night. When a Serbian man walked slowly toward us, we all tried to look normal. We took turns stretching and looking comfortable. He sat down beside us casually and made some small talk. His eyes were still and steady.

As he asked us how the morning was going, he handed us three plane tickets. We answered him, our eyes scanning the tickets. He nodded at our answers and got up to continue his casual journey through the small airport.

We were going to Sweden—not Stockholm, instead a place none of us had ever heard of called Karlstad. We knew of Sweden for its international reputation as a place that cared about human rights and freedom. We knew of it as part of the free world. It would be our final destination.

◆

The flight was short, only two hours. In that time, we decided in a frenzy of whispered conversations that it would be best if we destroyed all three of our passports. We would enter Sweden as refugees of war. We would slowly build lives in this place where none of us had ever been. How do three men each destroy three passports? What was our best option? We could think of only one plan: we had to take turns going to the bathroom during the flight. Each time, we'd rip two to three passport pages into tiny little pieces and flush them down the toilet.

Our plan wasn't a great one. We took turns getting up, lining up, going to the bathroom again and again. People started giving us weird looks. No one else had an opportunity to use the bathroom. Even the flight attendants wondered whether we were all right. Yes, yes, we were all right. Still, we kept on lining up and flushing the toilet and it was all getting very suspicious.

When the captain announced that we were landing and told us all to go to our seats, one of my friends whispered that he had not managed to destroy his third passport, the Spanish one. We could only feel sorry.

◆

The plane landed and we entered an airport the size of a medium coffee shop. The flight crew and the other passengers were all wary of us. The airport staff sensed their wariness. They asked all the European passport holders to stand in one line. My friend who had not managed to destroy his Spanish passport went into that line. I and my other friend waited in a corner with no idea what to do next.

When my friend's turn came to speak to the official, he was clearly nervous.

"Is this your passport?" the official said.

"No," he said.

The official looked at the picture of him, and said, "If this is not yours, is this your photo?"

"I don't know who the passport belongs to," my friend answered. He was so nervous by now that he could not look at anyone.

"If this is not your passport, how did you get it?" the official asked.

The truth came spilling out in a jumble of a story that was filled with tears and stutters and regrets and the people he'd left behind in Afghanistan and the reasons why he had to leave and how he didn't know what would happen next.

The official stopped him and calmly called over another official, who had already contacted the police. Soon enough, the border police arrived and took him to a small room off the main terminal.

Now all the passengers were looking at us in our corner. The suspicion on their faces made us feel even more pressured and I had a bad feeling. The friend with me bowed his head and went over to another official.

He said simply, "I don't have a passport."

I was now hiding behind a table, crouching. I know they must have cameras. I know the airport is the size of a coffee shop. I'm twenty-four and I'm so scared that I'm hiding in view of everyone looking at me.

A few of the border police came out of the small room to take my friend away. Meanwhile, everyone is looking at me and I'm still hiding.

Then I heard on the loudspeakers: "The person hiding behind the table in the corner, come out."

They spoke in English and I understood every word. I had to come out.

Officials surrounded me. They said a lot of things. I said nothing. They said more things. "I am not going to tell anyone anything," I managed to say.

They took me to another small room off the main terminal.

We were all separated now and there was no more knowing what each would say. I said that I was illiterate and that I didn't speak English or Swedish. They said, "No problem." They got an interpreter on the phone, a woman's voice speaking without emotion, just like a computer.

For the next two to three hours, they questioned me. One police officer offered me something to drink. He played the good cop. He said, "I want to help you." Another one, someone who looked like an immigrant himself, was the bad cop. His feet knocked my feet under the table. He said, "If you lie, you go to jail." I grew very confused. What did they want from me? It was December. I had no jacket, just a T-shirt. I sat shivering and I told them everything I knew, but it was not enough. Every time I told them a truth, they asked me the same thing again in five or six different ways. I recognized that they were interrogating me and using different techniques, and that it was not about them being mean or kind, they were just poking into me, pulling me apart.

As they asked and asked, I started thinking, *I'm not going to remember my responses. I'm not going to be able to repeat myself any longer.* I felt sorry for myself, so sorry. I was not a criminal and yet I was being treated like one. I started getting angry, too. Who is responsible for my situation? What had I done? What makes them better than me, the ones asking the questions, the ones with the power to make me shake and quiver? What was going on in this little room in the middle of Sweden? What was happening to me? I started to cry. I could feel that I was giving up, giving up on me, on my story, on my life in my country, on the chance of my life anywhere else.

I started asking the questions. What is the difference

between you and me? What is the difference between you and the people with the guns? The exhaustion was hitting me. I hadn't slept in a long time. I felt a terrible exhaustion expressing itself in teary hysteria.

I tried to control myself. It was better to keep asking the questions than to let the answers come from the actions and words of those around me. I thought, *I know what real humanity is, and it is not this.* I thought, *Is this how you would want people to treat your family and your children?* But the tears would not stop falling. Without being able to respond to their questions, and trapped in the thoughts that came to me in my despair, eventually all I could do was chew my lip.

At long last, they said that I had cleared security and the interview was over; however, the government of Sweden was not yet satisfied with my presence or my story. The officer who played kind gave me a bus ticket for the Arlanda Airport in Stockholm, for another interview scheduled at eight the next morning. He opened the door to the little room, and I saw that the main terminal outside was empty.

It was a dark night. It was a long night. The bus stop was right outside the airport. I was wearing only a T-shirt. So I waited inside as long as I dared before I chanced the cold. I had no other options before me—no money or paperwork, no connections. The traffickers had fulfilled their duty. The colder I got, the more I thought. What are all these white people doing in my country talking about humanity when this is how they receive the lost human beings? I looked into the darkness of that night, trying to find answers in the clean sweep of white snow.

The bus came in the early morning with its white headlights shining bright. Inside, it was already full of people. There was an empty seat close to the driver. I sat there. At each stop, I asked, "Where is the destination?" in English. The driver was nice enough. He answered quietly, "Your destination is the last stop."

No one on the bus spoke to each other for the two-hour trip. Everyone sat alone, huddled in the warmth of their clothing. The silence on the bus, after the commotion of the past few days of my life, was eerie. I did not want to look at anyone because none of them were looking at me—despite the fact that I was not dressed for the weather, that my face was stained with tears, haggard, and fearful. I saw how beautiful the country outside was. I saw men and women standing at the street corners, speaking politely, behaving respectfully. The lovelier it was outside, the more lost I felt inside.

I remembered the final ride to the airport in my country, the broken mud walls and the holes in the streets, the hunger of the people, the desperate men trying to patch the walls, find some security in what remained. More than anything, seeing no children that morning traveling to Stockholm, I thought of the many children in my country, the helpless wandering orphans. How was it possible that we lived in the same world? How was it possible that they were living like this and we were not?

I settled into the warmth of the heated bus. As it rolled along the street, making its hiccupping stops and starts, I started wondering, *Will this be my new home?* Then I was embarrassed by the thought, because where was my family, my siblings? How were they all?

I don't know what would have happened to me had I

learned then and there that shortly after I left the country my father had disappeared. He was on his way to the grocers and never returned. My family waited, and when he did not come back, they went in search of him. But there was no sign or trace of him to be found. It was not hard for them or for me to guess what had happened to him, but to guess would be to accept his fate and mine, connected as they were. Had I known that my leaving would mean his disappearance, I would not have done it. I would have died an honorable man in my country. I did not know, though, so I had left hoping for the best. Sheltered from the truth by distance and opportunity, I met my fate as bravely as I could.

Arlanda Airport was huge. While it was not as opulent as Dubai's airport, the scope and the scale of everything made me feel very small and poor. I couldn't figure out where to turn, to the left or the right, to go forward or hold myself back. I asked person after person, "Where is the migration office?" They gestured with clean hands. I followed those hands. Finally I found it. There were two other people ahead of me sitting in the waiting area. I waited for four or five hours before my name was called. I should have been hungry but I wasn't.

In another little room, I sat with two officers. They were not the men from the airport in Karlstad, but they played the same roles. In the maze of their questions, each asked from five or six different directions, I quickly became a fumbling mess. They asked me for my date of birth. I could not manage. I did not remember, but instead of saying that, I made up a birthday. What? When? How? Is that what you said yesterday? I started crying again, and I could not stop. The voice on the phone, again a woman interpreter, was void of emotion as she waited for my tears to cease, and when they didn't, she waited some more.

After the second or third hour, they said, "The interview is done." They handed me a bus ticket once more, and told me to go outside and to wait for another bus. This one would take me to a place where I could stay, a refugee holding center in the middle of Stockholm. All I could do was hold the ticket in my hands and nod.

At the bus stop, it was not long before another big bus came. Inside, there were lots of other refugees from around the world. I could tell by their clothing that many were from Eritrea and Syria. They, too, were scared, but they traveled in groups and appeared more confident. At the time, Sweden was offering 100 percent residency to Syrians and Eritreans. I looked at the family groups, children and men and women, and thought, who had been bombing us for forty years? Was it not Sweden, the United States, England, and their Western allies? Are these other refugees better than me? I was assaulted by my own sense of inferiority and anger. I felt so bad and hurt so deeply that the feeling lives on inside me, even now, in this moment. I thought, *I need a certificate of my humanity.*

That bus ride felt like it was two to three hours, but it was actually no more than thirty to forty-five minutes. The migration office in Stockholm was a big building right in the heart of the city. It was a temporary refugee camp, a holding center, they called it. We were put in a waiting area where I sat for two to three hours more before they called my name. I remember thinking the whole time: You cannot think of your hunger or the cold. You cannot.

When at last I was called into another interview room, I

faced the same interview, different people using the same techniques, the woman interpreter's voice on the phone, waiting patiently for my tears to clear and my voice to emerge. At the end, they handed me a heavy bag filled with toiletry items, a blanket, a pillow, and a change of clothes. The official said, "Choose a last name?" I was dazed but I would not be anything other than what I was. "I am Afghan," I said. The official waited for me patiently, then repeated, "Choose a last name." I chose mine. My last name. Achekzai. He typed this into a computer and printed an identification card. He gave me a piece of paper with a room number on it. Someone led me to the assigned room.

Inside the doorway of the room, I saw three beds. A man was lying on a bed with his hands over his face. I stood for a moment, then said, "Are you my roommate?" He lifted his arm off his face and turned toward me. It was my first friend, the one with the Spanish passport.

He leaped from the bed, and I ran to his side, and we cried and embraced like brothers, like countrymen. Still caught in our great reunion, we heard the door open again. We turned to see that it was our third friend, clutching an identical bag of toiletries. All three of us held each other and talked in a rush of our miseries since we were parted.

At five in the afternoon, we were called to a large cafeteria. Everybody in Sweden eats dinner at the same time. Suddenly, the hunger came over us. The food was good. It was great. We all eat Halal and were not sure if the meat was prepared accordingly, so we ate salad and potatoes and we were happy, thinking this is perfect.

Back in the room, my friends and I spoke more calmly,

even began thinking about what might happen to us next. Finally, we were all in Sweden, a part of the free world, and we were together in the same room. We shook our heads, overwhelmed by the strange feeling of not being able to place ourselves. Were we dreaming? Is Sweden a dream? Is Afghanistan a dream? Were we real? Too exhausted, we fell asleep quickly in our beds.

At eight a.m., breakfast was served. It was just like a restaurant in a hotel of refugees. There were Syrians, Eritreans, Russians, Serbians—much of the world was in that cafeteria, so much of the world, and then just us three Afghans.

One of my friends said he wanted to go out and walk around and see Sweden. The two of us were weary, so we retired to our room. We were talking quietly when there was a sharp knock on the door. An official stood on the other side.

She said, "Get ready, you are leaving and going to a more permanent camp."

We said, "What? We have a friend. He went outside."

The official shook her head, and said, "We have to go."

◆

We were taken to another place outside Stockholm, a refugee camp that had once been a five-star hotel and resort, owned by a smart businesswoman who decided to sign a contract with the Swedish government. When we arrived, we were greeted with hugs and a lovely welcome, the welcome we had all been afraid to dream of. The staff were trained to greet the wealthiest people in the world, so that was how they treated us.

The name of the place was Skebo Herrgård. It was a series of big manor homes around a small square, framed on one side by a rushing river and on the other by the tall mountains of Sweden. In the middle of winter the lawn was covered in snow. All the walkways had been carefully plowed. The trees stood reaching for the sky with their bare branches. A bright sun shone. It was the Christmas season, and whether you celebrated it or not, the mood was everywhere and you could not help but feel it.

I was there for two to three years. We didn't go to school or work. We ate, slept, had fun, walking everywhere our feet could take us. It was the most beautiful place I had ever been. In the spring, the river gushed and rippled over the rocks. The birds sang their mating songs. The wind blew warm breath on our sorry, hurting hearts. We could drink as much coffee as we wanted. The chef and the staff prepared beautiful meals for us; they smiled and greeted us warmly. But we were lost in the free world, floating particles. We were not normal. We couldn't trust anyone. Yet our surroundings were so peaceful, we felt as if we were in a strange kind of hell. Everything that had mattered was gone. I prayed secretly. Perhaps we all did. No one wanted to be identified as a probable terrorist, so we prayed hiding in our rooms. We prayed for a return to what was and a future that could be. We were held in a place that felt as if war didn't exist, in a world that we knew was fraught with fighting.

My friend and I were placed in a room with the only other Afghan in the camp, a young man who was trained as a pilot in Italy and had refused to return to the motherland when war broke out. He was a great liar. He'd get things donated from Swedes and tell us that he'd bought them. He was older than me and the kind of man who wanted the people around him to feel indebted. At first, we believed his claims, but he was not a careful man, so soon enough we realized what was going on, but we let him live his lies anyway. It was a reminder of a human tendency that was familiar in the strangeness of Skebo Herrgård.

When the opportunity came to apply for asylum in Sweden, I took it. My application was denied. I applied again. In fact, I appealed to the Swedish Immigration Court, challenging the rejection, citing how the United Nations office was not responding to my letters, how the Red Cross said it could not help me, how no one in the free world wanted to offer me safety. I challenged it on the basis that, from Afghanistan, I had believed in the promises of peace proclaimed by the democratic nations of this world and worked on its behalf, and now I was left homeless.

I was on a mad quest. I watched YouTube and I taught myself Swedish. My ability to speak English and Swedish made me much beloved by the other refugees in the camp. I could help them fill out forms. I could translate what other people said into refugee-speak. They started calling me, in a joking way, "Baba Teresa." In that capacity, I could ask the lovely hotel staff the questions that had been bothering me since my arrival: How do I improve my humanity? I said, "If I am human, what is my right? How does a human being, biological in every way, get documents of their humanity?" It was not long before there was enough concern that I was sent to see a psychologist.

◆

The camp psychologist got to know me well. At first, she was unsure about my mental health. She was baffled by my request for a certificate of my humanity. She asked me if I believed I was human. I said of course, but other people weren't so sure, so I needed help proving my humanity. She then offered to provide me with such proof. "But why?" I asked her. "What is the difference between you and me? How come you are more human than me, in a position to observe and certify my humanity? After all, did we not have the same blood, the same makeup? The same dreams, even? Why are you more successful in your humanity than I am in mine?" I told her that if she was going to give me a certificate of my humanity, she would have to show me hers first. I had to know who had given her the authority to determine human certification.

I had been a human in my country, a human in a war. I told the psychologist that the war was a war on terrorism but I was not a terrorist. I told her about the warlords, the communists, the religious thinkers, and the powerful humanitarians all doing battle in my country. I told her that I was just a human being and that many of the human beings in my country hate war. We were victims of war—to be specific, of the Americans and the Russians and their allies and their battle for power over people. She listened to me and took notes. Finally, she said, "You are not sick." She was then the first in a long time to say, "Thank you. Please come back to talk to me so that I can learn from you."

I would not have returned to her office if it was only for her to learn from me. I was also learning from myself. I was in so much pain, and my pain was so focused that I was unable to learn from myself. It took her taking the notes during our meetings and then reciting them back to me for me to know what I was saying, thinking, and feeling.

My dependence on the psychologist got me thinking about Sweden in a more general way. I came to understand that if I stayed in the country, I would be dependent on the government for a long time. It took eight to ten years to get citizenship, assuming that my appeal for asylum was accepted. I started thinking about being independent again, being the maker of my destiny, the maker of my life. I began thinking about America.

◆

I connected with my USAID supervisor, Natasha Kelly. I asked her once more about the Special Immigrant Visa. I applied. With Natasha's support and verification of my history, I made a case for coming to the United States, the source of so much hurt and so much hope all over this world.

On Facebook, I started asking political questions, demanding a response to my question on humanity. I asked again and again in long rants for a person who could grant me, and my country folk, the gift of a certification of humanity. One day I got a response from a woman, an activist in a place called Minnesota, asking me for my story. Her name was Diedre. In the span of a week, we became friends. After learning of my story, she offered to help me with the visa process.

◆

It was springtime once more in Skebo Herrgård. The birds sang their songs. Refugees walked in groups of two or three on the green lawn. I was talking to a group of Eritreans, helping explain some concept about life in Sweden, when one of the staff walked over to me and handed me two envelopes. The first and the bigger envelope was from the US embassy. Inside, there was that long-destroyed Afghan passport, made new again, its blue cover firm and stiff, and then a letter granting me US residency. The second letter was from the Swedish

Immigration Court, granting me Swedish residency. I started crying. We all did, all of us refugees, so hungry for some hope of a place to make a home. My fellow refugees from around the world decided they would have a big party for me with cake. We jumped. We danced. We hugged. The big question was, Which country to choose? They had both chosen me, on paper, at least.

I thought of my family. I knew I would have a better, easier life in Sweden. But if I went to the United States and worked hard, then I would be able to send money home, as much as I could earn. I thought of my mother, my baby brother, and my sisters in our house, now I've learned without my father. For them, I could not trust my fate to a country. I had to take it into my own hands once again. I chose America.

On Facebook, Diedre asked me where I was going. I told her about New York City or Washington, DC. She said, "Why not Minnesota?" I asked, "Is Minnesota even a state?" I told her to give me five minutes. I googled Minnesota. I saw that it was indeed a state, and that it was in fact a state in the heart of the country. I wrote her back and said, "Will you help find me a host?"

Within three days, I was set to leave. After a brief Skype call with a lovely woman named Gayle Denicker, I had a host family. One of my Swedish friends who worked at the hotel gave me a loan to pay for a one-way plane ticket to Minneapolis–St. Paul International Airport. Another friend at the hotel, seeing my empty pockets, placed a twenty-dollar bill in my hand.

◆

I arrived in Minnesota in June 2015. Gayle and her husband and Diedre and her husband met me at the airport. As they drove me to their home in Minneapolis, I heard police sirens. I saw homeless people with their bags and shopping carts beside them. I saw broken concrete and uneven sidewalks. I thought, *I've made a mistake. How can America go into the world and speak of humanity, of peace and prosperity, when there are so many within its own borders looking for help, searching for meaning, worth, a chance at a good life?*

◆

In America, I work sixteen to eighteen hours a day. During the week, I am an office manager at a community college. After work and on the weekends, I am a Lyft driver. I live modestly in a small apartment. Every dollar that I do not need, I send to my family in Afghanistan. It brings me pride. Because of me, my family is middle class, they have food to eat, my baby brother can go to school. Because of me, they are not lost in Afghanistan. Someone in America sees them clearly and loves them completely. I have been in America for three years. I am now twenty-nine years old. I am engaged to a woman my mother has chosen in Afghanistan. I've not met her but I know that she has a master's degree in Islamic studies. Will I be able to sponsor her and marry her here? I don't know. I don't know when a life will begin beyond this one where I work hard and take pride where I can.

In this life, I have learned that Afghanzada is as much a human as anyone else in this country or any other; I am as human as you are.

—Afghanzada Achekzai

Part III

PLEASE REMEMBER

9

Officially Unconfirmed

♦

IF I HAD a picture of me then, you would see that I was a boy with caramel-colored eyes and short curls on my head. My legs were thin and my arms were long. If I'd had a camera, you'd see: a boy taking deep breaths of the dry air, raising his arms high over his head and then letting them fall down. The dust that swirls in the clearing would look like turmeric in the wind. I didn't have a camera, so there are no images of myself from then, no scenes from my boyhood but the ones I carry inside.

♦

Every day, once the animals had been cared for, I played a game of soccer with my friends in a field of short grass on the outskirts of our village until the sweat dribbled from our faces and our chests started aching. It was then that we would go rest in the shade of a big tree at the field's edge.

We were country children from Eritrea. We were used to life in the wide openness of the old farms. We were good at taking care of the animals, setting the cows out to graze by the river, herding the bleating goats along the dirt roads to new patches of green, and being by ourselves.

For fun, we scared the hens that pecked at the bugs in the weeds by pretending to run at them. We would not do this to the hens with chicks. That would have been too mean. We had a code of conduct we lived by: we should have fun but be kind. My friends and I obeyed this Christian rule at all times.

◆

My mother died when I was just four months old. She contracted malaria. Without proper treatment, a recovery was not possible in the rural farms of Eritrea. She left my father with two sons, my older brother who was three at the time and me.

My father did not know how to take care of us, especially me. My grandmother took on the responsibilities of caring for me. I knew her as my mother.

I believed my grandmother was my mother until I was eight years old. I grew up believing that my father was my older brother, that we shared the same parents.

◆

I was just a child and I loved the warm blowing wind and the bright sunny sky on my heated skin. I took deep breaths to slow my beating heart from the soccer game, then made my way to my place beneath the canopy of leaves to sit with my friends. My best friend rolled the soccer ball toward me. My hands were young, plump, and full.

That fine day, the other boys left us to go attend to their chores. It was just my best friend, Adam, and I sitting beneath the umbrella of the leaves of our favorite tree, looking at the yellowing grass of the open field. The cows with their sharp horns and bony backs grazed in an uneven line along the slope of a hill. We sat in the dirt, scratching at our thin legs. The mosquitos had been fierce that morning when we'd taken the cows out to graze.

I told Adam that my big brother was coming back from

Asmara, the capital city, soon, and that he would no doubt have candy for me.

I told him about how lucky I was to have such a good brother, one who loved me so much.

My best friend was a sensitive boy just a year older than me, a kind kid who was always gentle and honest, but his look grew pensive in my talk, his brow furrowing.

I said, "I don't understand why my brother loves me so much, but he does."

My friend said, "I know why he loves you so much, Michael."

I said, "How do you know?" He looked a little nervous, so I prodded him, "Come on. You can tell me anything. We are best friends. What do you know?"

He said, "Michael, your big brother is really your father."

I said, "What?!" Then I started laughing. Who did he think I was? I shook my head. I slapped the hard ground beside me with my palms. The orange dust flew around us.

My friend waved his hands in front of his face to carry the dust away and said, "Michael, I've never lied to you. Why would I lie to you about this? This is serious. I heard my mother and an auntie talking about it. They were wondering when your grandmom would tell you the truth."

My laughter was gone by the time the dust had settled. My best friend was being mean, not at all being a good Christian. I let the silence grow between us. My throat grew thick. I could not fathom what he thought he was doing, making this cruel joke.

The landscape before me swam in a pool of sudden tears. I tried to blink them away.

I said, "No, you misheard, Adam. My mom is my mom. My dad is my dad. My brothers are my brothers. We are a family."

He got up, wiped his hands on his shorts, looked down at me, and said, "Michael, I'm sorry, but I know what I heard and I'm your best friend and if I didn't tell you the truth I wouldn't be. I think you should go talk to your grandmom."

I got up, too. I told Adam I would talk to my grandmother and then I would visit him later when our chores were through to let him know that he'd misunderstood. I handed him the soccer ball. He accepted it. He nodded sadly at me, his head bobbing up and down slowly, his mouth in a tight line.

We walked away from the tree together. There was nothing left to say to each other. We parted ways in the village. I looked at his back, shoulders low, head to the side, walking with both his hands holding the soccer ball in front of him.

At the open door to our house, I waited for a moment, looking at the older woman tending to the fire with a stick, a pot boiling on top of the flames. Her familiar hands moving steadily from one task to the other, unaware of my presence. The tears I had blinked away filled my eyes once more. Wet streaks ran down my face.

From the doorway, I said, "Mom?"

She turned immediately toward me.

She said, "Yes, Michael?"

She saw that I was crying. She rushed toward me, wiping her hand on the scarf tied to her waist.

She said, "Michael, what's wrong? What has happened to my boy?"

She pulled me close and I could smell the spices she'd been cooking with on her clothes. She was making *zigni* for dinner.

I could smell the spice of the berbere, the ginger, the cumin, and the cloves. I held tight as I leaned my head into her soft, familiar body.

I mumbled into her clothes, "My best friend said you're not my mom. Adam said you're my grandmom. He is a liar."

My words turned into a wail. Her hands pulled me tighter to her body for a moment, and then I felt them loosening. She took my arms in both hands. Normally she would say, "That is nonsense, Michael," but that day was not a normal day. In her growing silence, I knew what I would find when I looked up. When I felt her hand gently cup my chin I shook my head for a moment.

In the wash of my tears, I saw the face I loved most in the world, its soft lines folded into brown flesh, eyes darker than my own, framed by wrinkles, looking down at me with a look of sorrow.

Tears filled her eyes. She shook her head—as surprised as I was by the moment before us. A hand went to the base of her throat as she cleared it.

She said, "Michael, my dearest boy, your best friend Adam is not a liar."

She pulled me toward the pot of beef simmering in tomato sauce on the hot fire.

She said, "Michael, come inside and we'll talk."

When we were both seated, she used the same scarf she'd wiped her hands on earlier to wipe the tears away from her eyes.

She said, "Michael, I didn't want to upset you. I have wanted to tell you but I didn't know how."

Those words were the needle that pierced me through. My

muscles grew soft. I curled physically into myself. I mourned the death of my grandmom as my mom. I felt for the first time the loss of the woman who had given birth to me, the woman who was my mom but had never been in my life. Grandmom's voice flowed past me but I had lost all ability to hear her words. I was young and I could not understand how her love for me and my love for her would not change despite the knowledge that had fallen upon me beneath that cloud of leaves where my best friend had offered me a truth I had not been looking for.

When my immediate sadness passed, I noticed the flood of "sorry" on my grandmom's face. In the light of the day, her face sagged. Her mouth was open but there were no words. Her eyes, half covered by wrinkles, shone with her tears. It was I who reached for her then and said, "Don't cry, don't cry. You're my mom. Don't cry."

The conversation that day did not change my life in any remarkable way and yet it was and it remains the point at which I knew I was not like my best friend or the other children in our farming village. The knowledge set me apart and cemented a new and lonely perspective I would have of life and death.

My father, when he returned later that day, brought candy for me as I knew he would. When he handed it to me and hugged me, I buried my face in his neck and I held on to him tighter than I ever had before. His arms held me close.

He said, "What's going on, Michael? What's going on?"

I shook my head, refusing to say anything.

It was my grandmom who informed my father of our conversation earlier in the day over dinner as we gathered around the big plate at the center of the table to eat the *zigni* and injera bread. My granddad sat with his head bowed in a soft silence as my grandmom talked. In the evening light, they looked old and weary and defeated.

Berhane, my older brother, looked from my grandmom's face to our father's expectantly but our father showed no reactions. Once grandmom was done sharing the story, my father reached a cool hand to hold the back of my neck and said, "It is okay, Michael. I am as I have ever been. I am both your father and your brother. I will always be this way—just as your mom will always be your mom even though she could not raise you, and your grandmom will continue to be your mom because she has raised you."

My older brother, Berhane, nodded as if he had known the truth all along. His thin face and big eyes with long lashes made him look like a camel. He sat up straighter and made himself older than me by saying, "Yes, Michael. Everything will be all right."

Later, in our shared bed, I asked Berhane if he had known all along. He gave me a mysterious answer: "I kind of knew everything and I kind of don't all at the same time. Don't be sad, Michael. We love you and God loves you and we will all take care of you until you can take care of yourself. Then maybe you'll even take care of all of us."

Whether Berhane knew it or not, his words that night would become a charge I'd strive my whole life to live by: to live with the love of those around me and that of God, and to do my very best to take care of the people around me as I had been cared for. In some other world, without the kind of love that my grandmom and my granddad and my father and my brother and what my stepmother would eventually show me, I would have died along with my mother many years ago. But I was very much alive with my gratitude and great loneliness.

◆

I turned eighteen years old in that farming village beneath that fierce sun. Grandmom and Granddad were getting older. We needed money. It was not asked of me but I offered to move to Asmara to become an ambulance driver so I could send money home and help support my primary caretakers in their old age. By then, my father had remarried and had seven more children so I knew whatever money he earned had to stretch far.

My grandmom was worried because she had a feeling that hard times were coming for Eritrea, but I had been a farm boy, removed from the political happenings of the big city. I was eager to be part of a bustling city, doing good work to help people who I believed would share the same fate as me: survive despite the circumstances around them. I told Grandmom not to worry.

In the country, I had not paid particular attention to the mood of unrest in the realms of government. From school, I had learned both Amharic and British English, so I felt an assurance that I could communicate across different groups. If I couldn't, there was still the simple fact that I was a harmless person, a man out to earn some money to take care of my elderly grandparents only. I was young and strong and willing to work hard, so I was more concerned about our poverty than politics.

In my ambulance, I drove around Asmara admiring all the buildings outside the car windows. In 1890, Eritrea had been colonized by the Italians, so the architecture of the city of Asmara had been developed in accordance with their tastes and technological capacity. During Italy's effort to take over Africa in the 1930s, the very best Italian architects had worked hard to re-create southern Italy in Africa. The streets were lined with storefront cafés and wide sidewalks; the buildings were covered with tiled roofs beneath the towering palm trees. The city was filled with cathedrals and mosques. Each piece of architecture was a reminder of how far I was from the farm.

◆

I fell in love in Asmara. At twenty-three, I met a young woman named Lete. She was nineteen years old. She, like me, came from a humble background. She was in the city working hard to support her mother just as I was working to support my grandparents. Neither of us had much money but we were both hardworking and we were both tall and slender, so we believed we were each other's best chances for a beautiful life. Beneath a windswept sky of blue, Lete and I made a decision to be together forever, to get married and have a family, to make the best life we knew how for each other. Love, when a person's options are limited by finances, can be very straight-forward and honest.

◆

A year after our marriage, in 1974, the hard times that my grandmom had feared found us in beautiful Asmara. In my family, personal tragedy struck. My granddad died. He was only sixty-eight years old. In my country, the quest for Eritrea's independence had turned bloody. In the aftermath of World War II, the United Nations had declared Eritrea as part of Ethiopia, but we did not feel we were one people. We Eritreans wanted our independence and the Ethiopians wanted to continue their hold over our country. In the big capital city, only one massacre is on the books but there were more than that. Beyond the massacre of December 28, 1974, there were others.

Before the massacres, we were both consumed with the fact that Lete was pregnant. Her belly grew round and her face soft. We had visited my grandmom to warm her heart and her hearth for the Christmas holiday. We were full of thoughts of Mary, Baby Jesus, and the blessings of Christ.

◆

On the morning of December 28, 1974, I was in my ambulance, making my slow way toward the hospital to report for the day's work. I loved my morning drives in Asmara, the buildings around me peaceful and sleepy in the rose-gray dawn. I turned my ambulance around the street corner, expecting nothing out of the ordinary, just the routines of early morning: students walking in groups, café owners sweeping their front walks, the merchants transporting their goods.

As I turned the corner, I saw something I had never seen before outside the hospital walls and in the churches: I saw dead bodies.

The photograph in my head is black and white. It is of twenty-seven students, men and women, strangled to death with piano strings. There were some with faces, gray as the pavement they rested on. Others with heads hanging by a thread of skin. The bodies were littered about the alleys and the doorways in a mess.

My eyes were drawn to the faces. I stopped the ambulance, knowing it was all too late for me to do anything.

From the ambulance, I studied first one face than the next. I was sure I had seen them alive at different intersections, walking, laughing, and talking around the city, boys and girls in well-ironed school clothes. Now those very same clothes lay wrinkled and wet against their limp bodies. Their feet, which had been going places, were stiff and still, pointed in different directions.

I said to myself, again and again in the car, "Michael, your job is to attend to the living."

I put a hand to my heart and said, "Michael, your job is to witness their deaths."

Small groups of silent people gathered around the bodies.

The whole of the city had grown abnormally quiet. We had all become mutes. Even the cars around me had stopped making their noises. The birds? Where were they? The children? Were they not hungry or upset? Everything had stopped for those young people.

I told myself, "Drive, Michael. Drive to the hospital. They might need you there."

My lap was wet with fallen tears when the driving was done, and at last I was in front of the hospital. My eyes were open but the camera inside my heart was stuck on the images of the students.

◆

On another day, off the record, I drove through another street lined with pillars of bodies. They had been killed by wires around their necks. There were men, women, and children. Their eyes were half closed and half open, bulging.

Fear was precisely the reaction that the Ethiopian government wanted.

On yet another day, at the hospital, a general barged in through the doors. He wore army fatigues. He had on boots.

A hat. A gun. He towered over the head doctor, a thin guy with thick glasses who shook out his words one at a time, like a sputtering engine, "I will, I will, I will not document your seventy-six dead bodies on the streets in my hospital records. My job here is to document the deaths within my hospital. It is the job of the government to record the deaths of those they kill. I am not going to write anything down for you. It is against international law."

The general stormed out as he had barged in. He'd brought cold air into the hot room. We felt the chill of his visit only upon his exit.

For four years, we lived this way. All the while, the camera inside filling up with images that could never be erased.

◆

By 1978, Lete and I had two young daughters. They both had my eyes. When my daughters looked up at me, I saw pools of warm caramel spilling sunlight. We named the oldest Hadas and the younger one Mahta.

I'd never seen a photograph of my mother. None existed. But the moment my grandmom and my father saw Hadas, they both said, "That is your mother's face and your mother's eyes looking at you, Michael."

I had not known that I had been looking at the world with my mother's eyes. I gazed at myself in the mirrors and my daughters before me and pieces of my mother slowly appeared in my life. The loss that I had believed was absolute became something else, something more mystical and magical.

Mahta, unlike Hadas, had her mother's calm about her, a softer, rounder face and serious eyes, perpetually thinking. In this way, she offered me a glimpse into others I had not known, considerations that were new to me.

Lete and I loved each other, but our children were our most sacred gifts and responsibilities. From the moment I became a father, it was as if my heart had turned into liquid inside of me. I felt love in my arms and my legs, my fingers and my toes. Everything I did, I did more gently than before, from the way I handled the patients, alive and dead, to the way I drove a car, made a turn, stopped, or started the ignition of the ambulance.

In every conversation I had with my grandmom after the girls were born, she said, "Michael, you have to take your beautiful children and leave. You have to go somewhere where they can grow up and know peace in their hearts, smell the clean air and lift their faces to the bright sun."

The place she wanted for my children was the world of my youth. We could not return to the past, so I looked for possibilities in the future. I knew people were fleeing to Sudan, but I knew my grandmom would never leave Eritrea. I could not choose between the mother she had been to me and the father I would be to my daughters.

One evening, when we returned home for a visit to the farm, after dinner as our family sat talking in the gray evening light, listening to the wind blowing through the fields, far away from the chaos that had become life in Asmara, I tried to talk to my grandmom about leaving.

I said, "Mom, if I leave Eritrea, will you leave with me?"

She said, "Michael, I want to go back to my home village when I was a child far from here."

She said, "Michael, I see so much in my mind for you and your family but I don't see myself with you all in this happy future."

She said, "Michael, if you stay here, you will die for me. Do you understand that if you go, then you will get to live for me?"

My grandmom had a different kind of camera clicking away inside of her. It was a world in which my daughters would live free and happy.

On my last day in Eritrea, I packed clothing and food and I sent my grandmom to the village where she had been a girl. There, we had an uncle who I knew would take good care of her. At the uncle's house, my grandmom took a seat by his fire. Her face was illuminated by its flames.

She said, "Michael, be careful."

My grandmom reached for me with both hands. She kissed my face, on either side. Then, she hugged me—much as she had done when I was a child.

In parting, she said, "Don't cry, Michael. Don't cry. Even when I die, you just pray for me and that is enough. Your work taking care of me is done. Now, your work is to take care of your children. God will always be with you, my son."

◆

On my last day in Eritrea, I saw no deaths but I knew that the only mother figure of my life would die without me there to comfort or care for her, this grandmom of mine who had mothered me with love and patience. By the time I returned to my family, thick clouds had fallen low in the sky. Although it was early in the evening, the world outside was dark. Lete had packed the children already. She placed Hadas on my back and I placed Mahta on hers. We secured the children to us with fabric. Then, we ran in the heavy downpour toward the forest.

Our goal was to get to Sudan. Once we were in the thick of the forest, the rains ended, washing away whatever footsteps we might have left. We settled in a small clearing. I knew the journey would take three days.

In my arms, Hadas was restless.

She said, "Daddy, I want to go home to my bed."

I offered her a blanket.

She said, "Daddy, I don't want to sleep in the dark."

I made a fire.

Mahta cried. Lete gathered her close and breastfed her in the light of the fire I had made.

That night, Lete and I dared not talk. We searched the heavens for the things we wanted to say. We found the dark clouds parting and the stars shining down.

In the morning, we made it to a desert town. I negotiated for some camels to take us northwest toward Sudan. We met other refugees making the two-day trek from the villages of the highland through the deserts. We were kind to each other, recognizing that we shared the same plight, all hopeful that Sudan would welcome us as refugees.

◆

In Sudan, we made friends with a family of Eritreans who'd left earlier in the conflict. They gave us food and shelter in a town close to Wad Sharife Refugee Camp. I did not want to move my family into the crowded camp but I knew I wanted to work in it.

With my experience as an ambulance driver and ability to communicate in English and Amharic, I got work with the

American Red Cross. My job was to drive the doctors from town into the refugee camp, to drive around sick patients, and to drive the medical supply trucks when necessary.

Every day more refugees streamed in with their hurts. The doctors did what they could to treat what they saw, but the wounds they couldn't see went untended. While there were no physical war wounds on me and I was not sick in body, my heart ached and the camera inside of me kept playing the reels of the people dying on the streets of Asmara again and again. There was no relief to be found inside of me, so I pushed all I had into the work outside of me.

Lete and I were able to find a little house for our family. We did not have electricity or running water but we made do with what I earned, feeding our children and keeping them in school. We lived in Sudan for nine years. In that time, we had three more children: Helen, Yoself, and Mehret. Each offered me a connection to a past that was bigger than me and a future I hoped fervently to see.

In that time, my father came to visit us. He was sick. He died during the visit far away from the farmlands of his boyhood and mine. Beneath a hot sun, in the desert sand, we buried the man who had been as much a brother as a father to me.

In Sudan, I learned that beyond the guns and torturous murders committed in warfare, when a country fights, it must do so on all fronts; diseases were rampant in the conditions of our lives.

In 1985 and 1986 there was a big cholera outbreak in the refugee camps across Sudan. While the outbreaks remain officially unconfirmed—just like the continuous killing of civilians in Asmara—I was there and I lived through it.

In the refugee camp, at the height of the crisis, there were twenty-five thousand people sick with cholera. The disease did not discriminate among the poor and war-stricken population. On the hospital beds, men and women and children lay head to foot, side by side writhing in agony, or so quiet and still and depleted they appeared dead. The people were like tubes: what we put in one end flowed out the other. In the camp hospital, doctors and nurses and all medical personnel were called to attention. We ran down the aisles doing our best to respond to the cries and the pleas of the sick and those who loved them. The stench of vomit and diarrhea, of human sweat and fear filled the rooms, and the flies flew in swarms of black.

The sick people sat, if they could, hands holding their tummies and their heads. Those who could not sit slept on the beds, skin and bones disappearing beneath the clothes they wore. Their eyes were closed. Their eyes were open, holes in the skeletal faces. They stared without seeing. Sounds of human suffering abounded, day and night, with the endless buzzing of the flies.

In those two years, all of time became the suffocating moment, the frenzy, the crazy, impossible task of helping the sick ones make it through the painful process, one way or another. Near the end of the epidemic, the refugee camp hospital had no more gloves. We, lower level workers, handed the doctors in charge the gloves we could find. None of them took the gloves from our proffered hands. They shook their heads, too busy for words, and gestured for us to put them on. Sweat dribbled down their faces, dark faces glistening in the heat of battle, once pale faces now flushed red. The United Nations doctors saved the gloves for the nurses and the ambulance drivers like me. They worked without gloves, around the clock, through the night and the day, to save the people. Only seven hundred people died because of them.

I promised myself then that if I had money one day, I would give it to the United Nations doctors. What they did in that Sudanese refugee camp saved a part of me that was in danger of dying. I had seen how people could take lives in Asmara. In the despair of the camp in Sudan, I saw how people could give life, and somehow in this knowledge, my dreams for humanity were saved.

My daughters don't know how the wind blows in the farmlands of Eritrea. They don't know that once upon a time I was a boy who grew up believing I had a mother because I had my grandmom's love. They don't know about the camera I never had but the pictures my heart carries.

All they know is that their father is getting old. They say he is a good storyteller.

◆

In 1991, two years before Eritrea won its independence but just as the war was ending, I became an American citizen. The *Star Tribune* came to the ceremony. They published a picture of all of us new Americans. Of all the hands that were raised, mine, an old man's hand, crooked and bent, skin with lines of white fanning out in all directions like a web, was the highest. It was God that I was speaking to, thanking him for loving me, my family, and my people and showing us that peace is possible if we hold fast to not only the bad stories but the good ones. Life is too short for just the bad to happen—even in a hard life.

—MICHAEL TESFAY

10

Natalis: Same Old Tired World

THE WOMAN LAY on the sofa, her head on its leathery arm, her cell phone in her hand. She'd put on weight. With each breath, her stomach rose, a soft mound of flesh beneath her polyester shirt. She needed a haircut. Her black hair, kept short, had grown long, its strands covering her eyes like a teenage boy's. Her hair hadn't been this greasy since the years when she'd worked the night shift and then spent the days caring for her young children. She had used the time she had to wash her hair for sleeping instead. She looked sluggish, sagging flesh and clothing, sitting on the sofa, her iPhone in her hands.

The woman spent all her time looking at flowers on the Internet. She knew how to find and save the photos, flowers everywhere, from around the world, the tulip fields of Holland, the orchids of Thailand, the beautiful Buddhist lotus ponds, the purple heathers abloom on the English moors. Once she saved the photos, she passed the days editing them, changing the filters and cropping the images. She had over eleven thousand pictures on her phone.

Sometimes she was afraid. She saw black things the size of cats move across the living-room floor. Her eyes frantic, she made no sound. Instead, she froze in place, her only movement her eyes helplessly searching for an exit from her body.

She had vivid dreams of handsome men who came into her life on horses. They all wanted to marry her and take her away. In the dreams, she wanted to go with them, except she couldn't quite lift herself off the ground and onto their high horses. Her body was heavy in the dreams, anchored firmly to the earth. Sometimes she woke up reaching for the handsome men only to feel the empty, lonely air of their absence.

She couldn't sleep at night without the drugs. Even with them, during the day she was tired, drowsy, had no heart for anything or anyone.

Sometimes, she cried for her dead father. It had been nearly half a century since his death, but to her it was fresh as the morning. She believed she knew where he was, always at the edge of the horizon. There he waited for her with wings like the birds. He sent messages to her. He offered a promise to lift her up high so they could soar through the skies together. From there, he told her, she wouldn't miss her children because she could still see them on earth.

Most of the time, though, she spent her days on the sofa looking at her phone. She did not have the energy to cook or clean, two things she'd always attended to as a matter of life and death for her children.

In the past, no matter how little sleep she was functioning on, she made traditional meals for her family, with no store-bought sauces and little fat. She boiled fish with lemongrass, tomatoes, green onions, cilantro, mint, basil, red hot chili peppers, a touch of MSG, and then salt to taste. She made bowls of rice with tofu and chicken soup. Her children loved her mung bean thread soup with minced pork and green onions and cilantro, black pepper galore. As they ate, she would stand at the sink waiting to wash each plate, bowl, spoon, and fork. Now she herself was never hungry and her children's hunger held no power to get her up.

All her life, no matter where they were—in the refugee camps or the housing projects of Minnesota—she and her husband's bedroom was a place where the bed was always made, the floor clean, clothes folded in baskets, hung in closets, stored in drawers. No matter the mess beyond its doors, the chaos of the unsteady world was never allowed to enter. Now she'd place a blanket on the floor. The mountain of clean clothes that needed to be folded and put away was nearly as high as their rumpled bed. Now the dust of their lives had settled on her body and grown so thick she could barely move.

Her husband, used to the woman from the past, perhaps hoping that she would return in light of the current conditions of their room, did not pull the covers over the sheets in the mornings or sit to fold the clothes, so the pile grew higher and higher.

At the doctor's office, the nurses gave her evaluations. Worksheets designed to see if she was healthy or not. The questions asked if she was feeling any pain in her body; if yes, where? On a scale of 1 to 10, how much did she hurt? How often did she hurt? Was the pain less or more than at the last visit? The questions asked if she had energy for the daily work of the living. Was she able to focus on a book or a television show? Was this more or less than at the last visit?

Each time she answered "the same," the doctors increased the dosage of her medication. When one prescription did not work, the doctor shifted to another. The woman was put on Wellbutrin, Prozac, Zoloft, Paxil, Effexor, Cymbalta, and more.

One pill made her believe that she was on the cusp of death. Her heart started racing. She grew short of breath. She spoke her death wishes: keep the funeral simple; I don't want my death to be complicated.

At the doctor's office, on the suicide question, she shook her head adamantly, and said, "My biggest fear is that I'll die and leave my children behind. I would never kill myself."

She wept.

The doctor asked why she was so sad.

She answered, "I don't know what to do with myself. I am out of work. I'm too young to be useless. My children need a mother who can take care of them."

The doctor wanted her to go out into the world. Yes, she could no longer find a job with her shoulder being so bad, her disability documented, but perhaps she could volunteer in a community organization? She couldn't drive. She didn't speak good enough English. Her hands hurt. Her feet hurt. Her neck hurt. She was falling apart. The doctor said she could not change the conditions of the woman's life; the only thing she could do was change the conditions of her head. No one knew what to do with her heart.

Her fiery heart. The heart of the only girl in her village to go to school, to race ahead of the boys into the classroom. The heart of the young woman who'd chosen love in a war full of death and despair, made a decision to live in the face of death. The heart of the mother who would place each of her children, alive and dead, before herself with no misgivings or regrets. The heart of a wife who did everything hard so her husband, in a world that had given up on him, could not give up on her and their life together. Now her heart hurt.

The pills made the woman so tired she could not fret about going out into the world. They numbed her body so she could not feel the pain in her hands, her feet, her neck. They glued her together inside a bubble of despair. The doctor could not change the conditions of the woman's life, but she made it so that the woman could live with them.

Each day, the woman floated further and further away, in a bubble of flowery images, framed and filtered. One day, the bubble rose high, a brisk wind blew, and it lifted far into the clouds of another world. The woman became a shining particle in the wide openness. This was, of course, her fondest fantasy.

In actuality, her doctor referred her to Natalis. Its name sounded like a planet, but it was a medical office on University and Snelling Avenues, one of the busiest intersections in Minnesota. The office was housed in a large green building with a clock facing the intersection. Its architecture looked like the big Lego buildings her children built when they were younger. When her family had first arrived in Minnesota, she'd visited the building because there was an office in it that gave food and clothing to poor families. She had come here then, a young refugee mother with little ones holding fast to her hands, to see what was available in the food pantry, if there were coats that would fit the family for the approaching winter. It had been many years since the woman had been in the building. While the outside looked the same, the inside had been remodeled. Instead of the old nondescript wallpaper of the 1980s, there were now large ceramic tiles set into the walls and new pillars rising high.

She saw that the people sitting on the chairs in the Natalis waiting room were no different than the ones who had visited the food pantry decades ago, except now there was even more variety of newcomer, men in *salwars* and women in hijabs, men and women with brightly woven handmade bags she recognized from parts of Southeast Asia. Most everyone had an interpreter with them, younger people busy looking at their phone screens or filling out forms.

The waiting room was a big rectangle. There was an island in the middle where patients registered upon arrival. There was a small line of patients waiting to be registered. The woman looked nervously around the room, unsure of how to move.

A plump young woman in jeans, a pair of heels, and a dark sweater came up to the woman: "I think I'm your interpreter." The woman nodded. Although her daughter had driven her to the clinic, times were different now, and most clinics and hospitals preferred professional interpreters. It was easier this way. She didn't want her daughter to be the one to repeat in English everything she might say to the doctors, depending on their willingness to listen or what they wanted to know.

The young interpreter had messy hair. There was the remnant of a child's sticker on the back of her head, clinging to her dark hair. Her sweater was stained with streaks of dried white, probably children's snot. Her fingers were thick, her nails half painted. She wore red lipstick. She smiled and said, "I'll sign you in."

The woman took a seat in the waiting area. All the chairs were too high for her short legs. She swung them beneath her in time to the sound of the validation stamper. The woman folded her arms around her purse and waited. Her daughter sat to her left, trying to make small talk. The interpreter joined them, sat a seat away, and brought a form to fill out. The woman admired her surprisingly legible handwriting—unlike her own daughter's. The interpreter's fingers held fast to a black pen and ran over the questions softly.

"What's your birthday?"

"You're a refugee?"

"How long have you been in America?"

"You don't work anymore?"

"What did you do when you were working?"

"You were an assembler? Just like my mom."

It was this offer of information that made the woman smile unexpectedly. Her teeth, stained by time, were strong. They gave her face something hard to contrast the softness; they gave her a piece of herself back.

◆

I liked the young woman with the uncombed hair. I asked her what her last name was. I asked if she was married and whether she had kids. My daughter gestured toward me and when I leaned close she whispered in my ear. "Mom, you're not sup-posed to ask her so many personal questions. She needs to be a professional." I moved my ear away from her words. I was tired of all these young people telling me how I'm supposed to act in America, what is and isn't proper.

The interpreter said, "You're just like my mom. She comes here, too. Everybody comes here. All of you older people, when you were busy raising children and working, you didn't have time to think about the war and all the people you left behind. But now you're old and out of work, and you spend way too much time thinking about the past, it's made you sick."

I told her she was probably right.

Almost every person who had returned to the waiting area from the single door that led to the back offices had come out with crumpled tissues in their hands, their eyes watery and red. They weren't looking left or right or even straight ahead, but at their feet. One of my sisters-in-law had told me that the doctor she was seeing wanted her to go and see "a crying doctor." I realized that this may very well be where I was.

The realization made me uncomfortable. We, all of us in this place, were sad and broken. My sadness and brokenness made me embarrassed. I didn't want people I knew seeing me here. I had heard stories of other elderly refugees trying to con disability by pretending to be crazy. I had known such people in my life. One time a widowed neighbor had taken to licking her shoes at the doctor's office. Her back was hurting her, a bullet wound from the war, she couldn't work standing up at the factory anymore, and her kids needed time to grow up, so she had taken the only path she knew to survive in America. She pretended to be crazy. She'd told me how embarrassed she'd been but that her integrity meant less than the needs of her children. I, too, had lost my job and the outlook for my family was not good, but I wasn't ready to pretend to be crazier than I am.

The interpreter interrupted my thoughts. "They just called your name. It's time for us to go in."

I got up, still holding my purse in front of me, a weak shield against what was to come. and I followed her toward the door. My daughter followed me.

Inside, we found ourselves in a dim hallway. Around the corner, the nurse had me stand on a scale. I asked my daughter to hold my purse. I took off my shoes but left my socks on. I'd gained fifteen pounds in the last six months. I stood by the measuring wall, pushed my chest out, and leaned back. I'd lost nearly half an inch. My blood pressure was good enough. The nurse took the numbers down, the interpreter explained them for me, and then we were led into a small office. The big wooden desk in the room faced the window, so we sat facing the wall. The desk was empty except for a box of tissues by its edge. There were degrees with fancy letters hung behind the desk.

The nurse told us that the doctor would be in soon.

We sat quietly. My daughter and the interpreter both took out their phones, so I did the same. I didn't have Internet connection so I couldn't find more photographs of flowers. I opened up my old images and cropped the ones I'd already saved. I hated the photographs of beautiful floral landscapes that included people. I knew why photographers did that—so that years later, they could look back and remember. But they weren't me and I wasn't there and I only wanted to see the beautiful pictures of the flowers by themselves, uninterrupted by anyone else's intentions. I took a deep breath. My daughter looked at me with concern.

There was a knock on the door before a tall man in a white coat entered. He was the doctor. With him was a well-dressed and healthy-looking older woman. He said she was a resident. He introduced himself as a psychologist who specializes in working with physicians to prescribe medical interventions. He had a small file on me, but he sat behind the desk and asked me what was going on.

I told him the truth. I told him about the dreams. I told

him when I'd started taking the latest medication and what I was seeing. He listened, his hands clasped on the desk, looking at me occasionally and then back at his folded hands. He nodded thoughtfully when I finished telling him what was going on.

He asked, "You're still sad?"

I didn't have time to prepare for the tears. They bubbled forth. My hands reached blindly for the box of tissues on the desk. The doctor pushed the tissue box closer to my hands. I held tissues to my eyes and I nodded.

He asked, "Can you tell me why?"

I started to tell him my story. I talked about my mother and father. I told him that my father was already an old man by the time I was born, that he'd planted a huge orchard of citrus fruit for my brothers and sisters and me so that when he died, we'd always have a place to go and find the sweetness of life. I told him that my mother had been an orphan and had grown up without a mother's love and that she'd always wanted to be kind to her children, and that she had been the kindest mother to me. I told him that I was only sixteen years old when I got married and I had to leave my mother behind, because my father had died when I was just eight. I wanted to tell him about the war, but I could see that he was looking at the watch on his wrist, so I stopped.

He smiled kindly at me. I looked to the well-dressed resident beside him and she smiled, too.

He said, "I'm going to up your dosage for your current prescription. You can continue taking the Trazadone to help you sleep at night. I'll see you again in six months' time. If you experience anything worrisome, call your primary doctor."

I nodded.

He said, "Do you have any questions for me?"

I couldn't think of any questions.

The doctor and the resident shook our hands. They smiled and they said they were happy to meet us, and then they left the room.

I followed the interpreter out of the office back into the waiting area. I could hear my daughter close behind. I didn't dare look at any of the patients in the waiting room; I kept my eyes down and my left hand firm on the wet tissue.

In the car, I took out my phone. I knew my place on the sofa waited for me. Even the thought of getting there slowed my breathing. I turned it on and let the flowers pull me away into places more beautiful than here.

—CHUE MOUA

11

Sisters on the Other Side of the River

MY WIFE, MY three boys, and our baby girl were about to cross the Mekong River, from Laos to Thailand. It was 1978. I had traded all our belongings for a small raft. I would not be able to get on the raft, but I could squeeze on my children and my wife, tie myself to it, and swim with the current. It was two or three in the morning when we made it to the river's edge.

I had been a Hmong soldier trained by the Central Intelligence Agency of the United States. We were told we had to fight communism. I was a young man from a family of farmers. I knew little about the different political groups of the world and nothing of the Cold War that was playing out in Laos. I had always thought that perhaps I could become a teacher as I had been a good student. Unfortunately, at sixteen years old I was drafted into the war by our village head. My father, a simple man, did not have the arguments or the means to keep me, his oldest son, by his side. While my mother and father cried the day I left for training, my own eyes were clear. I understood that my future would depend on my ability to learn how to be a good soldier. The alternative was death.

Once the training began, I quickly rose to the top of my class—if you could call us that, a ragtag group of farm boys.

Unlike some of the young men I was with, I was literate. I had gone to school, so I was fluent in Lao and had a foundation of French. English was not impossible to learn. I could understand the commands from the CIA officers working with us and follow the protocol of the Hmong men whose job it was to prepare us for war. While I could handle a gun, the men in charge saw that my best asset was my mind. They trained me in wartime interrogation tactics.

From 1960 until 1975, I interrogated prisoners of war for the CIA in a camp they'd set up in the Phou Bia mountains. I earned a regular salary, one that was enough to attract and secure the hand of a young woman I adored. Together, we started a family, uncertain of the outcome of the war. But by then the war had gone on for so long that we could not see an end to it, and we knew that if we didn't live, we'd die having never had a life at all.

Suddenly, in 1975, the CIA and the American soldiers just left. Their planes took them away as we watched from the ground, thinking until the very end that they would come back. The days turned into weeks and the weeks into months and the months into years, and our lives were nothing more than running away from the communists who had come into power and hunted us down like animals. By 1978, most of the boys I had trained with had been killed. I knew that if I were ever captured, my whole family would die with me. Our only chance of survival was to cross the Mekong River and head for the refugee camps in Thailand.

There was a full moon the night of our crossing. All along the river, families were preparing to enter the water. I had seen two little girls going from family to family. In the moonlight,

I could see the people shaking their heads at the girls. I prayed they would not come to us.

The older one was six or seven years old. Her scraggly hair fell about her face. She carried the little girl on her back with a length of cloth—the child was three or four but too weak to walk. In the older girl's arms she carried a small pot. The little one whimpered occasionally, raising her head weakly, turning it from one side to the other, seeking comfort. Her sister was quiet as she walked along the line of families. It was impossible to ignore them.

I had just blown up the raft and was tying my children together when the girl walked toward us. In light of the moon, reflected off the surface of the river, I saw her eyes, big and round in her sunken face. She offered what was in her pot to me before her words came out.

She said, "This is all I have left in the world, this little bit of rice and the little sister on my back. Our mother and father, our aunts and uncles and grandparents were killed in the jungle. We are alone. We've traveled for the last five days on our own to get here."

I said, "I can't help you. I'm sorry."

She persisted, "I will give you this rice if you carry my baby sister with your family to the other side. I know it is not much rice but it is all I have left."

I said again, this time with more roughness in my voice, because my children could hear her, "I'm sorry but there's no room on the raft."

The girl's thin arms shook with the proffered rice in the near-empty pot. Her little sister turned her head at the roughness of my voice to look at me. Those eyes, too, were large and dark like a little monkey's. They glistened at me, wet with tears.

The older girl fell to her knees. It looked as if her thin legs had given out from under her. Her head was bowed, and she begged, "Please, uncle. You don't have to take me. I'm willing to die here, on this side of the river. I would die happy knowing my sister is safe. Please, uncle."

I shook my head at her, my own words now wet and sticky in my throat.

The girl turned to my wife, who had our baby girl strapped to her front, and said, "Please, auntie, please."

She started to cry. We were the last family at the river's edge. Her cries turned into sobs.

My wife's arms tightened around our little baby's body.

We had had a three-year-old daughter. A year after the Americans left, in an abandoned village by a rushing river, she died in a drowning accident after a night of heavy rainfall. It was my wife who'd found her body, floating away from our house, her shirt tangled up with a fallen tree. After our daughter's death, we thought we would never have another little girl in our life. What spirit would choose parents like us? A man and a woman who could not protect their children? Our daughter had laughter like the songs of the birds and dark hair that blossomed about her face like a flower in bloom. Her tiny hands and feet had danced in the air when she ran, recalling the flight of butterflies. Her scent was fresh as the citrus blooms that fell about the orchard or the long grass after a night of light rain. Her soft touch was full of warmth. Her words contained vistas of possibility. All these were gone when she died. Still, somehow, in this horrible war, in the wet heat of the jungle, with the hunger and the fear, from up high in the sky, in her chase after the clouds, a baby girl's spirit had seen us and chosen us. Our new one entered our life healthy and strong. She gave us faith and strength to continue our long trek through the jungle, to this riverbank, with our boys.

I stood in front of the girl on her knees and my shaking wife. I said, "Little girl, we have to go into the river now. The soldiers are surely coming. You take your sister and you go hide in the jungle. When other families come, you ask them. Someone will help you. We can't."

Her shoulders shook with her cries. She had no more words for us. The rice in the pot was in danger of spilling. I took hold of it with my hands. I put it down beside her. I said to my boys and my wife, "Hurry up."

I turned from the girls and I pushed the raft into the river. I picked up my boys one by one and dropped them onto the raft. I helped my wife and our baby daughter, strapped to her front, onto the raft. The flimsy thing nearly toppled. I could hear the other men hurrying their families into the current. A voice called out, "The soldiers are coming."

I felt a tug on my shirt. I had hoped the girl would have walked away, taken my words to heart, found a place to hide. I had hoped hopelessly. She'd stepped into the river after me.

I did not have the heart to pry those fingers loose, so I said, "I'll come back for you both. I promise. As soon as I get my children and my wife to the other side, I will turn back for you. Just wait here."

Her fingers fell from my shirt. My wife echoed my words to the girls. My children, too. I turned to the girls one last time and placed my hands on each of their heads, a sign of love. I looked into their eyes and I believed myself. I would come back for them.

The water was cold against my legs. The cold climbed higher as I walked farther into the river. My feet lost touch with the river's bottom. I treaded water. I kicked water.

Somewhere at the halfway point of the crossing, floating in the Mekong River, I clung to the raft and looked back at the girls. I could see they were still standing in the river, both staring straight ahead, toward me. Their small pot of rice sat on the bank. Every few minutes, I looked back at them until they disappeared from view, until they were nothing more than lines of shadow in the moonlit night.

There was the cracking of guns from the tree line. The soldiers had arrived. I called out to the ancestors, the spirits of the earth and the water, to please keep the girls safe, to please let a better man than me come their way. I kicked at the water with everything I had and pushed toward the other shore.

On Thailand's side, we lay down on the soft bank of the Mekong River. My chest heaving, I looked up at the sky. The night was fading. The earliest hint of the morning sun was chasing the darkness from the horizon; slivers of pink, orange, yellow, and blue bled into the canvas of the heavens. My family was huddled on the soft dirt beside me. When I could, I pushed myself up. There was barely anything visible on the other bank, just shadows moving like men yelling into the distance, their guns in their hands. There was no sign of the girls anywhere, no little pot of rice to be seen.

◆

In Ban Vinai Refugee Camp, two years after we crossed the river, my wife gave birth to another daughter. Her arrival was the impetus for our departure from the camp. It gave me the courage to cross the wide ocean to find a better life in a foreign land. My family applied for resettlement and when the option was presented, we chose to go to France. I was more fluent in French. My wife and I never talked about the sisters on the other side of the river. We just held fast to our girls, promising ourselves that we would never leave them on a forsaken shore. We departed for France in 1981, our youngest secured to my wife's chest.

We lived in southern France for nearly twenty years. We joined the other Hmong refugees in Nice and Nîmes, where many of us made our living tending to the fields of lettuce, cabbage, and other vegetables. In France, one more little boy entered our lives. We raised our children, and they grew tall and strong like the carrots we planted in the fertile soil. We thought that we would live out the rest of our years in France, but in 2000 my wife decided that we had to leave France for the United States, where her elderly mother, her only sister, and her seven brothers had resettled.

The Twin Cities has the largest concentration of Hmong refugees in the world, and we joined them, to claim the extended family that we thought we had lost. Here in Minnesota, we opened a grocery store with our children, who all fell in love and married and had children of their own. It is a successful enterprise. People from the community come in and they say, "You are doing well for yourself and your family. You are a good man."

They don't know the truth. They don't know that nearly forty years ago, on the banks of the Mekong River, on my way to freedom, I condemned two sisters to war. They don't know that I cannot forget those two girls, their eyes that night, round like the moon in the high sky, looking at me. The lie I told. The lie I carry. They don't know that one day soon, when my time comes, I will look into those eyes again, and see the knowledge that I was not the man the sisters had been waiting for, that I could not be him. I pray and I hope that in another life, beneath a different moon, I will be the man to turn that raft around.

—FONG LEE

Part IV

EDGE
OF THE
HORIZON

12

A Burial and a Birth

SAYMOUKDA'S MOTHER, SANOUTHITH, had been sick with cancer for more than two years. She'd been placed on hospice care at her daughter Saymoukda's house after the last cycle of chemotherapy failed, when Saymoukda's father could no longer attend to her care by himself. On a brisk October day, when the wind blew the leaves across the street and piled them along the curb, a big truck delivered a hospital bed, a walker, a commode, and other equipment into the little house with the neutral walls. Saymoukda's family of three grew suddenly into a family of four, then five (when her father also moved in), and more as family and friends came to visit and stayed to help.

Sanouthith had been a vibrant woman with thick black hair that she wore like Farrah Fawcett's, layered waves flying away from her face. She'd favored bright red lipstick and a tad of blush on her high cheekbones. She'd driven a Jeep Wrangler. For much of her life, she'd been gifted with copious amounts of energy. The cancer came as a surprise. Its impact was devastating. After the first round of chemotherapy, Sanouthith lost her hair and the color on her lips and her cheeks, but more than these things she lost her vitality. After the second round, she lost her independence. Her face and limbs swelled with excess fluid that her body could not dispel as her system started to decline. In the hospital bed, in her daughter's house, she sank into the shell of her body.

Saymoukda spent countless hours beside the bed in a folded chair. Her young son, Akara, just two years old, laughed and played in the space around the bed that had taken residence in the living room. He climbed onto his mother's lap and made her laugh across the span of days. When he grew tired, he asked to climb onto the hospital bed to cuddle close to his grandmother. Sanouthith's arms, no matter how heavy, lifted for the warm heat of her only grandchild.

Watching the little boy with the curly hair and the full lips curled close to her mother brought Saymoukda great joy. Here was what mattered in her life, the two of them, one her day, the other her night; together her mother and her son made her world turn around and around.

◆

Sanouthith had been the daughter of a provincial governor in Laos. She'd grown up living in a white colonial-style house with big pillars on either side of its front door in the heart of Vientiane, the capital city. She'd been a basketball star at the Catholic school she attended. In fact, Sanouthith was so good that she'd been invited to play in a tournament in France—although her father declined the invitation on her behalf.

Now the body that she'd always trusted—even during the moments when her mind and her heart had been confused—was giving up on her. Now she herself was giving up on her body, bit by bit. The process was slow and it was painful.

Now Sanouthith lived closer to the days of old than those that dawned each morning across the endless gray, despite the twinkling lights of the Christmas tree that sat in the center of the room, the beautifully wrapped gifts underneath it. She knew Christmas was coming. Before Christmas, it would be her daughter's birthday. Sanouthith knew that the family was also in the darkest days of winter, that soon enough the longest night of the year would come. She wanted to leave before then.

In her final days, Sanouthith traveled freely between time and space.

◆

It was a different Christmas season. The children, Saymoukda and Aroundeth, were both young and excited by the prospect of gifts. Sanouthith and her husband had to go to work on the pine farms outside the cities to ensure that the much-wanted gifts would be possible. She took deep breaths of the cold air, scented by the cut pine. In the factory, with the bright lights overhead, she and her husband stood side by side along the edge of a long worktable. Around them, there were Hmong refugees, all doing the same work. Everybody was twirling pine leaves into wires, making Christmas wreaths. Her hands were thick and heavy with the dried sap from the trees.

Her hands were rough and raw.

The coldness she'd shivered from was replaced by incredible heat. The sun was burning down. She tugged at her shirt with heavy fingers. The field of cucumber vines spread out before her, lines of prickly green leading to the very edge of the horizon. How long had they been picking the tiny cucumbers? The pain in her back was unbearable. They needed the extra money to buy school supplies for the kids in the fall. Little Saymoukda with her bangs cut across her forehead and Aroundeth, so eager to grow up and become a man, both hungry for the fine shoes and the nice jackets.

She'd once had fine shoes and nice jackets. She'd once lived in a place that was never freezing cold or burning hot.

In the early mornings, along the French-style two-story houses, beneath the tall trees, lines of young monks walked in robes the color of the setting sun. They had a driver who took her each morning to the French school, where she and other girls of her class learned about the history of Laos and the languages of the West. The girls played basketball for fun and wore pristine white shirts throughout the day. What should she have for lunch? To walk toward the vendor with the bowls of thick rice noodles in pork stock or the sticky rice lady who sold banana-wrapped packages of steamed fish and spices?

The thought of food made Sanouthith unhappy. Her mouth was dry. She wanted water. No, she didn't. She didn't want anything. She wanted to sleep, to dream again. No sticky rice with steamed fish and herbs. No chili paste with pork skin. No soup with melon vines and dill and peppers. No water. Nothing, please. No more.

◆

No more killing.

No more war.

King Savang Vatthana, Queen Khamphoui, and Crown Prince Vong Savang had all been killed. They were now killing the governors one at a time.

Oh, no! What about my father? My father has left . . . he's left his children behind, all of us, my six brothers and sisters, my countless stepbrothers and stepsisters. He's fled on a boat for Thailand. From there, he's taken a plane to a place called Pomona, California. He sent a letter saying we all should leave, too.

By the time the war was over, I had finished college. I'd been trained as a teacher. I was working as a supervisor on a dam project. In 1978 I met your father. Saymoukda, your father was a water buffalo gangster boy with some college but no degree.

Your father was working on the dam as a construction worker. He was tall, dark-skinned, and had strong, thick shoulders. In the field, he did not stand out from the rest of the hardworking men toiling beneath the hot sun. It was not until your father and his crew needed more gas and oil for their machines and he came into my office to make the request that I noticed him. That day, he was happy, so he smiled at me. I saw the small space between his two front teeth and the lines that fanned out from his eyes. I noticed that the top of his left index finger was missing. He allowed his appreciation for the strong bones in my face and my athletic form to show. This was post-1975, the world we belonged to had toppled; the old walls had crumbled. We took a strong liking to each other, so much so that after a short period of seeing each other at work and after work, we married.

Aroundeth. Where is Aroundeth? Where is my son, my good boy?

The government was slowly seeking out and killing anyone affiliated with the old administration. They had begun interviewing neighbors and friends, keen on finding who my father's children were. We couldn't stay and keep our baby boy Aroundeth safe, Saymoukda.

Your father likes to say that we left Laos on a boat. He is wrong. We swam across the Mekong River. He doesn't remember like I do.

Saymoukda, we never drugged your brother on the run toward the refugee camps. Aroundeth was such a good baby. He was a year and a half old only. Each time there were soldiers nearby, all I had to do was pull him close and whisper, "Shhh, don't make a sound." He listened to me.

All of us made it out alive, and we didn't have to drug your brother, Aroundeth, like so many others traveling with little ones.

And you were born on December 24, 1981, in the refugee camp in Thailand, my beautiful baby girl, with my bones on her face, my shoulders, my arms and my legs. My daughter who will one day become an athlete, not play basketball like me, but fall in love with volleyball, and become so good at it she will get a scholarship to go to college. You made me proud from the moment you were born, Saymoukda.

There was Nok, little bird, little boy, little one who came after you. He was only six months old when he died in the refugee camp. I gave him a name with wings and he flew away from me, from us, all of us.

◆

There's a bird chirping across the still, winter's night. Is he calling for me?

Saymoukda, can you hear him, calling for me, his mother and your mother?

Saymoukda, your birthday is coming. The day you were born is almost here.

◆

Saymoukda had fallen asleep beside the bed. She cushioned her head on half of her mother's stack of pillows. Her husband, Akiem, nudged her gently. The shadow of him, tall and bulky, stood over the bed. Akiem wanted her to go to bed. But Saymoukda was now wide awake and the first thing she said was, "I'm fine here. You take Akara to bed."

Akiem assured her—as he had many nights these last several months—that Akara had long been asleep. He offered to sit with her mother, but Saymoukda shook her head. Her mother's breathing had been particularly labored. She would stay up and keep watch. Akiem honored her wishes. He gave her shoulder a squeeze, then made his way toward the stairs to the little boy asleep in the big bed waiting for him.

In the soft light of the Christmas tree, Saymoukda focused on her mother's face, traced with her eyes the strong bones that rested beneath the skin. The family was Buddhist. In the beginning, she'd asked for a cure to the cancer and a recovery for her mother. Now she found herself asking for grace and mercy, kindness for her mother's journey, for herself, and for her child. She was sad. The feeling was all too familiar, too old.

When she was a child, Sanouthith had often told Saymoukda, a gentle hand brushing at her bangs, "You were so sad when we got to America, Saymoukda. Do you remember any of it?"

Saymoukda had no memories of her own sadness, only her mother's.

◆

I was seven years old.

It was a lovely spring weekend near the end of the school year.

My mom and dad liked taking us on these short road trips in our family's tan Isuzu truck.

We'd explore Minnesota, drive through the fancy neighborhoods full of white people, head to the west side of St. Paul to practice reading Spanish on the storefronts along Robert Street, cross the Mississippi River on Highway 52 going south, and climb the surrounding hills, looking at the old, crumbling neighborhoods in Frogtown where the Asian grocery stores and restaurants lined the avenue.

On these drives, we stopped at local parks and playgrounds. Sometimes, Mom and Dad would sit in the car and listen to music, mostly Lao and Thai singers whose names I'd never known but whose voices I'd recognize anywhere.

That particular day, Dad took us to Highland Park. The car had just stopped when Mom got out suddenly. She slammed the car door behind her. Dad was silent. He took a deep breath and leaned into the steering wheel. Aroundeth looked surprised.

I felt I had to chase Mom.

Dad and Aroundeth watched silently as I opened my door and raced after Mom.

She climbed the hill. I climbed after her.

I called for her. She turned toward me.

I stopped, waiting for her to gesture me close or perhaps even to walk toward me. She turned away and started walking again. I could see she was crying. I chased after her some more.

At the top of the hill, Mom folded. Her legs seemed to have given out from under her. Her breathing was ragged when I got close enough to hear. She'd come to a sitting position, but did not look up at me. I stood in front of her. I didn't know what to say. I crouched down on my heels. I started picking at the grass with my hands.

Mom said, "Bury me here."

I said, "I can't. I'm only seven."

She said, "When you are older."

She started weeping then, freely. Her hands were at her side. Her head was bowed. Her shoulders shook. I allowed myself to sag into the grass beside her, my hands grabbing at the blades of grass and pulling them from the earth.

Mom never told me what she was sad about.

◆

I was still seven years old.

It was a dark autumn night. The wind howled outside. Cold rain fell on the roof of our house.

The house was full of people, our family of four and Dad's younger brothers.

I had fallen asleep calmly that night, tucked warmly in the knowledge that despite the weather outside, we were comfortable and dry inside. By the time I fell asleep, Aroundeth was already asleep, breathing deeply from his bed in the corner.

I was awakened suddenly. The overhead light was on. Mom was in the room, standing at the foot of my bed. Her hair was a mess around her face. My brother and I were not prepared for the glare of the lights or the sight of Mom this way. We both sat straight up in our beds in the mess of our room, toys and clothes, his sports gear and mine, strewn about the carpet.

Mom said, "Get up! Pack! We are going to Uncle's house!"

We nodded in dazed surprise. She had clean garbage bags for us. She put one on each of our beds.

She rushed out of the room, yelling behind her, "Get into the car when you are packed. We are leaving your dad."

In my disturbed state of sleep, I obeyed the sound of Mom's pain. I started packing my sleepover bag. I put in underwear. I put in an undershirt. I thought I needed jeans but I also wanted to wear a dress. I was very confused. It took me a long time, long enough that my dad's youngest brothers woke from their sleep, realized there was commotion, and came to investigate.

From the doorway, I watched Mom sitting in the car in the pouring rain.

I heard my young uncles telling Mom to return to the house, to sit down so the family could all talk. I remember my dad wringing his hands, not saying a word, standing silently by my mother's car, drenched and shaking.

He has never said anything to Mom in the wake of her anger and her pain. Not once in any of the moments I've ever witnessed.

I stood there, my garbage bag in one hand, until I heard the engine of the car go quiet, saw its lights go dark. Aroundeth was sitting on the floor beside me. I told him that we could return to our room.

In our room, Aroundeth fell asleep quickly. I listened to his deep sleep, saw the dark of his empty garbage bag on the floor. I waited for the sound of the front door closing before I curled into a ball in my bed, unsure how to process Mom's overwhelming sadness.

◆

If there was a single reason I feared growing up, it was the simple fact of what my mother had said to me that day, her request that I bury her when I grew older. I tried to stretch out my childhood.

◆

One summer, Saymoukda spent every minute she could lying down in a blue plastic pool her mom and dad had gotten for Aroundeth and her. She'd just lie there and leave the hose running until the pool filled with water, until the water spilled over the sides, soaking the grass, inviting the fat worms out from underneath the ground. She would look at the bright sun and, when it grew too intense, close her eyes and stretch out her arms wide on either side, pretending she was in the ocean floating away.

Growing up, Saymoukda made friends with other refugee kids around her neighborhood, lots of Hmong kids and some Vietnamese kids, the other poor kids of color who lived in the houses with peeling paint, lots of African American and Latino American kids. They came up with elaborate schemes for fun and food. In the summers, they walked to neighborhood cherry trees and crabapple trees, picking bagsful of the small, hard fruits. They kept watch over each other, coughing out warnings and signaling precaution with hands and feet when there were passersby. In different kitchens, they took handfuls of salt and chili pepper flakes and mixed them in their palms. They ate from each other's hands, dipping the tart, sour fruits into the salty-spicy mix, making faces at each other until their mouths grew numb. When the food-pantry trucks came, the children ran to line up for small bags of rice, expired baked goods, and chunks of yellow cheese. Once the trucks were gone, they went through their brown grocery bags and traded their foods for the things their families liked best. In Saymoukda's case, it was rice and rice and more rice. She gave all the cheeses away. With their bags full of the things they loved, they walked home to their families full of pride.

Saymoukda's parents wanted Aroundeth and her to do well in school. They sent the kids to St. Mark's Catholic School for a couple of years. It went horribly. The children didn't speak English well. They were learning, but they were learning with kids and teachers who could only see their difference. At parent-teacher conferences, the teachers often asked Saymoukda to interpret things for her parents. "Saymoukda is a nice kid but she likes to talk and make other people laugh too much." Instead of a clean interpretation that would cause her parents to worry, Saymoukda would interpret the hidden messages in the teacher's words: "Saymoukda is a wonderful kid who takes time each day to talk to the children around her and make them happy." The conferences went well, so her parents were happy.

However, when Saymoukda got older, she urged her mother and father to register her for public school so she could be with her friends from the neighborhood. They agreed. Catholic school, even with a scholarship, was expensive.

In public school, Saymoukda was placed in English as a Second Language support classrooms. She had a teacher named Mr. Smith. He was a nice man who enjoyed books. His favorite activity was to have his students read out loud for one another. Saymoukda did not like books, so reading was not her thing, but one day when it was her turn to read *Charlotte's Web*, she heard a few of her classmates snickering. The sound made her angry. Usually, a kid read no more than three lines. That day, Saymoukda read nonstop, subjecting all those other refugee kids in the room to the sound of her voice for the entire class period. She read two chapters of *Charlotte's Web*. It didn't matter what was happening on the page or in the story. What mattered to Saymoukda was the message she was sending: you don't laugh at Saymoukda Vongsay unless she wants you to laugh with her.

Laughter became Saymoukda's answer to everything boring, everything scary, everything sad, everything that had anything important to do with her life. She spent the rest of her education working on her ability to make people laugh, saying the things she knew would surprise people, or share some perspective with them.

For example, during a lunch break in high school, a Hmong girl told a scary story about a ghost in her family's home. Saymoukda is Lao and also believes in ghosts, so she was not questioning the girl's reality, but while all the other kids sympathized with her fear and nodded over her story with awe and interest, Saymoukda offered some advice. "If that ghost has any power at all, you better tell that damn ghost to give you the lottery numbers."

Saymoukda became a popular girl. She was athletic like her mom—in fact, her athleticism got her into college as a proud C student. Her ability to smile like her father drew people in—all kinds of people, white kids, brown kids, black kids, other Asian kids. At the end of high school, she was awarded letters in volleyball, track, and basketball. Saymoukda could not stop time; she could not stop herself from growing up and going places.

◆

I hated my time at the University of Minnesota–Morris. I hated that there was nothing to do in that little town. We had a cemetery on campus but I was not dead yet, so it wasn't useful. To fill my time, I started becoming active on campus. I joined the Asian American Student Association. We didn't do much and it was a shitty waste of time, but we wasted time together talking about Asian American spirit and Asian food and things like that. I even campaigned to become the group's president. I ran on a platform that we would focus on growing our membership, bring more people of Asian descent on campus to present, and explore Asian American identity on campus through planned programming. Although we were all young, I was beginning to build a network of political artists and activists. When we could, I had us come down to the Twin Cities to attend the open mics. There were no Lao poets, but I heard people like Bao Phi, David Mura, and Ed Bok Lee. They were all men, but they were the ones making the noise so I crowded close to hear what they had to say. My continually wanting to leave Morris and my hunger to hear more diverse voices was how I met my partner, DJ Kool Akiem.

It was my junior year of college. It was a Friday or Saturday night. I knew I had to study for midterms. My friends wanted to go to a concert. I thought that maybe the concert would be in town or in Minneapolis, maybe on First Ave. I loved hip-hop and they said that it was a Rhymesayers tour, so I was in. I said good-bye to my books. I grabbed a jacket and got in a car with them. We drove and drove and drove, and by the time I knew we weren't anywhere close to the Twin Cities, we were good and settled in North or South Dakota, in a hotel banquet hall with big old chandeliers hanging from the ceiling and the lights turned low. Akiem was in that room, a DJ on that tour.

We got into the banquet hall and my friends dispersed. We were hard core, so we had our own preferences for positions at concerts. I always stood near the back of the venues. In the event of a fight, I wanted an easy escape. I was just settling into the vibe when I noticed that someone was staring at me. I moved farther and farther from the gaze. Half an hour later, I found myself still moving and this person still following me. I decided to go outside for "a breath of fresh air."

It was a hip-hop concert. Lots of people were outside, everyone taking "a breath of fresh air." I found a place where I could lean against a wall, hear a filtered beat thudding through the cement. I was just preparing to take my own "breaths of fresh air" when Akiem stepped close. He asked if he could have "a fresh air" with me. I shrugged and shared. We started talking.

He noticed the stamp on my hand.

He asked, "Why do you have a stamp?"

I didn't know it then but he was ten years older than me. If he'd ever gotten such stamps, it was too far away for him to remember. I wasn't yet twenty-one.

I asked, "How come you don't have one?"

He shrugged and said that he liked my stamp. I licked my

hand and I stamped him. He laughed. Then he said he had to go back inside. His "fresh air" break was done.

Ten minutes later, I returned to the banquet hall. I saw Akiem was onstage. I realized who he was. I knew his work. I knew he was a music producer in the Twin Cities. In fact, we had a common friend, my boyfriend at the time. After his set, he came down and found me at the merchandise table.

He asked, "What do you want?"

I said, "Everything."

He said, "Fine."

He got a bag and gave me one of everything from the merchandise table. The, he handed me the bag. The air in the banquet hall had grown thick and hot. The chandeliers above sent shimmers of light across his face. He asked me for my number just as I noticed that my shoelace was untied, so instead of answering him, I handed him my purse and bent down to tie my shoelaces. By the time I got up, my friends had found us and it was time to return to Morris.

He said, "Can I have a hug?"

I asked, "Why?"

He said, "I might not see you again."

I said, "Sure," and spread my arms wide.

In the hug, he again asked me for my number, and in that hug, I gave it to him.

A few days later, back at Morris, sitting at my desk, I got a call from Akiem. He told me that he was on his way to go to a movie with a friend, another rapper whose work I knew.

I could hear the rapper ask, "Who are you talking to, Akiem?"

Akiem answered, "My girlfriend."

The rapper informed him that I was already dating their
mutual friend and that Akiem better back off.
Akiem laughed in response.
I found myself doing the same.
Laughter brought me love.

◆

Laughter brought Saymoukda new life.

In 2015, Saymoukda got pregnant. On a hot August day, she and Akiem were working in their shared studio in downtown St. Paul. He was recording music. She was reviewing notes for a play. They'd just learned weeks before that Saymoukda was three and a half months pregnant.

That day, the summer sun filtered into their warehouse and dust motes floated in streams of light around the pair. Outside, embedded into the circles cut from concrete, there were thin trees with leaves of dark green reaching in the direction of the sunshine.

It was a surprise when Saymoukda felt sudden cramps across her middle. At first, she didn't want to disturb Akiem, so she shifted positions, went from standing to sitting, to lying down, first on her back and then on her sides. It didn't matter what she was doing; the cramps were steady and grew stronger and stronger. She texted a friend. The friend assured her everything was fine. She tried to believe the friend. She started bleeding. The bleeding grew worse. The cramps grew more painful. Finally, Saymoukda told Akiem. He suggested positions she'd already tried. In her heart, the truth dawned slowly.

It took her body all afternoon to realize what was happening. It was around four in the afternoon when the truth slipped out into the toilet, a dark glob of blood the size of an egg, or an avocado pit. Saymoukda held her hands over her middle, her legs shaking on the toilet seat. She wanted to scoop it out. She wanted to bury it. Instead, she flushed the toilet. The sound of the water flowing into the bowl, the swirl, the twirl, the lifting of the blood of the baby, the whole of it, is a sight and sound she will never forget.

◆

In 2017, Saymoukda got pregnant again. She found out when she missed a period. Her mother and father were not home. They had returned to Southeast Asia. It was their first time back. On the Internet they shared a photograph of the two of them standing in front of the dam where they'd first met.

In the photograph, they look healthy. Her father is balding. He has on sunglasses, so his eyes are hidden. He stands beside her mother, his left shoulder behind her right. He's still broad and strong-looking. Her mother stands beside him. Her own shoulders are less broad, the skin of her arms sagging in the sleeveless shirt she wore that day. Her eyes, hidden behind an even darker pair of round sunglasses, must have been piercing and direct: deep, dark, and unafraid. Her father is smiling in the picture and the space in between his two front teeth shows itself, like an open door to a closet. They look like tourists, not two people visiting a piece of their personal history.

When Saymoukda saw the photograph, she thought: *Mom and Dad are older than that dam behind them.*

While her mother and father were in Laos, Saymoukda messaged them from Minnesota to share news of the pregnancy.

When her parents received the message, they visited a temple on a mountain. They climbed its high stairs, holding to the railing made of concrete, the long run of a dragon's back. They stood underneath a tree of golden leaves, foil-covered coins, and bowed their heads low, held their hands together at their chests, to ask for a kind soul for their grandchild, a healthy spirit. A gentle wind blew just then and gold-foiled leaves started flying down. The coins jingled. Her dad opened his hands. A single leaf fell right into his upturned palms. For Saymoukda's parents, lifelong Buddhists, this meant that the baby would enter into the world on the fallen leaves of gold and land gently into the hold of those who loved him. A monk at that same temple gave Saymoukda's parents a name for their grandchild: Akara, one who was full of knowledge and compassion.

When her parents returned, the family discovered that Saymoukda's mother had cancer. Chemotherapy was an option, so they took it. As Saymoukda's body changed with the pregnancy, she watched her mother's change, too. Every day she grew fuller with life as her mother diminished. Saymoukda's hair grew thick and lustrous. Her mother's thinned and fell out. These changes were not lost on either of them, but both held on for the promise of a next generation.

The October before her mother was put into hospice, Akiem and Saymoukda were scheduled to close on their first house together. On the morning before the closing, Saymoukda started to feel contractions. Akiem wanted to go to the hospital, but she did not. Saymoukda wanted to go to the bank. They needed a cashier's check for the closing scheduled for the next day. The bank didn't open until 9:00 a.m. It was only 8:40.

In the empty parking lot of the bank, they sat waiting in their car. The sun was brilliant, and the leaves, already turned, glistened in colors like sandstones on the trees. Saymoukda kept calm by doing deep-breathing exercises. She thought about funny things but found she could not laugh. She thought about sad things but discovered she also could not cry. By the time a security guard unlocked the doors to the bank, Saymoukda was hunched over in pain.

Akiem supported Saymoukda on their walk into the bank. He held her firmly by his side as she requested a cashier's check from the teller, a young, unsuspecting woman. Every few minutes, the contractions came coursing through her body, causing Saymoukda's breath to grow short.

The teller smiled and asked, "Are you okay?"

Saymoukda nodded. "Yes, we are just excited about this check."

At half past nine, Akiem and Saymoukda were on their way to Woodwinds Hospital.

By eleven, Saymoukda was officially in a room. The pain would not stop but the baby would not come. She requested an epidural. Akiem stood beside her and read the baby monitor again and again. The day slipped into night. The night turned into a new day. The morning and then the afternoon passed. Saymoukda insisted that her parents come only once the baby had been delivered.

It was one p.m. the next day when the doctors finally told Saymoukda to push. She pushed. She pushed for the miscarriage she had experienced and had not yet surfaced from; she pushed for her mom and dad, the life they could have lived in Laos, and the one they had created in America; she pushed for that little girl who was afraid to grow up, for the old woman she hoped to one day become, for this little baby who was on his way into her life, and for the woman not yet old who was now sick and would die.

Akara was born, healthy and not so happy, at three p.m. His face was round. His head of hair was curly and wet against his scalp. His eyes were fiercely closed and his fists raised high above his head. Saymoukda called her mother and father, and all she could do was cry. In the background, Akara cried with her. On the other end of the receiver, she heard her mother's cry in response.

At five p.m., Akiem went to the closing by himself with the check Saymoukda had insisted they get the day before and secured the keys to their little house.

◆

Two years later, in that little house, on December 20, 2019, at 5:57 a.m., before the winter solstice, Saymoukda's birthday, and Christmas, Sanouthith passed away. A beloved sister, her husband, and her daughter were at her side. There was no laughter, only tears.

For much of Saymoukda's life she had been preparing for her mother's burial. She did not know that she was also preparing for the birth of a new generation. Saymoukda could not have known that the stories of her refugee past, the moments of her youth, her ability to find laughter on the edges of her tears would be the foundations of her art and her life.

—SAYMOUKDA DUANGPHOUXAY VONGSAY
In loving memory of Sanouthith Vongsay
December 12, 1952–December 20, 2019

13

Revival

WHEN MR. TRUONG bought the building in the early 1980s, it had seen better times. The two-story brick structure on the corner of Avon Street and University was built in 1922. While its façade of red brick looked good enough, inside, the interior was old and crumbling. The musty smell of dust and mildew was heavy in the air; old windows let in gusts of cold wind. The wooden windowsills were rotten with mold.

When his family of immediate and extended relatives expressed concerns about the state of the building, Mr. Truong insisted, "This is a good location for a restaurant."

The old man was not wrong. The building was located on what had once been the busiest street in Minneapolis and St. Paul: University Avenue. On one end stood the Cass Gilbert State Capitol Building with its gilded horses, and near the other end, on the banks of the Mississippi River, on the border of Minneapolis and St. Paul, the sprawling University of Minnesota's Twin Cities campus. However, the old business corridor, like the building Mr. Truong had purchased, had seen better days.

The streets were littered with trash. Along the sides of the buildings, there were empty syringe needles and used condoms containing traces of what looked like clotted cream. Up and down the avenue, there were sex shops and XXX theaters. The police sounded their sirens through the stretches of night, from dusk until dawn. The men, women, and children who traveled the streets early in the mornings and late at night looked over their shoulders, walked with their chin tucked low and shoulders high. There were some who could barely walk straight, so drunk or high or both that they had to hold the sides of the buildings and the light poles for support, zigzagging up and down the avenue. Sometimes, their heavy heads led and their feet could not follow and they fell flat onto the crumbling sidewalks, snores rising from the crumpled bodies. It was one of the roughest parts of St. Paul. The local people called the area Frogtown—for the frogs that had once lived in the long-ago swamps in the area and the guns that continued to croak through the night.

Mr. Truong recognized something that his oldest son, Hai, was still too young to see: that the neglected and abandoned avenue was not without hope or humanity. Perhaps he knew what the boy would discover in time: University Avenue and the refugee experience had a great deal in common. Both could not escape the hard times, both would survive.

University Avenue had been grand in the early 1900s. In 1913, Henry Ford had two plants on either end of the avenue building Model Ts. During World War I, Moses Zimmerman had operated the largest horse brokerage in the region and was the largest supplier of horses and mules to the US government. In the 1920s, the avenue was home to the largest streetcar network in the country, with more than five hundred miles of track. In 1939, Louis Armstrong played on the stretch, at the

Coliseum. For a time, the avenue was home to two of the finest restaurants in Minnesota, the Criterion and the Blue House.

But like all else, the street was not immune to change or the forces of the world. World War II ended the era of the streetcar and ushered in the age of buses and family cars. Cars and buses made it easy for wealthier families who could afford them to move farther away. Working-class people moved in. When Interstate 94 was built, whole neighborhoods were demolished. The corridor was full of abandoned buildings that had once serviced those who could pay for their goods. By the time Mr. Truong bought the old building, the people he was able to attract to the restaurant were other poor folk—many of them new Americans like himself, immigrants and refugees, whose old countries and wars that had brought them to America were often absent from the history books and the consciousness of the American public.

Without meaning to Mr. Truong had put forth one of the biggest questions of his son Hai's professional life: Was it ethical to make money from people without money?

The older Mr. Truong was not concerned with such philosophical questions. He, like many of the small-business owners, refugees, and immigrants slowly moving to St. Paul and setting up shop on University Avenue, was struggling with more elemental questions: How do I keep my family alive and build something that can be ours in this new country? They were leading a wave of small mom-and-pop businesses opening along the avenue: car repair shops, groceries, and small restaurants. They were able to operate by cutting corners where they could. They all hoped to garner customers by sharing their skills, their favorite things from their home countries and home tables, to run businesses by putting to work their whole families, including kids like Hai.

As the eldest son in the family, Mr. Truong was responsible for the family's well-being. He rallied the extended family for the work of renovating the dilapidated building. Mr. Truong made an executive decision to move the door from its place in the corner to the very front of the building. When questioned, his response was simple: "Easier to see from the University Avenue, easier to call the people in." The family set to work in the kitchen, scrubbing the decades of scum off the floors and the walls, scaring the rats out into the back alleys with pots and pans and knives. Mr. and Mrs. Truong got everything they needed for the restaurant from secondhand retailers: tables and chairs, plates and bowls, spoons and forks—all except chopsticks and Chinese soup spoons with their short handles and deep, flat bowls, because these things, like the new refugees and immigrants who used them, were new to Minnesota and no past retailers had ever used them before.

As the oldest grandchild and son in the family, Hai followed Mr. Truong closely on his days off from school and over the weekends. His job was to relay information to the younger generation and provide immediate support when needed. The restaurant was the most important family endeavor the Truongs had ever embarked on. Hai understood the stakes were high. He knew the family's livelihood depended on the restaurant's success and that the leading force of it was his father. He worked hard to support Mr. Truong with jobs big and small, from helping carry furniture and arranging it, to prepping ingredients for the test recipes his father wanted to try.

Mr. Truong set an easy menu, one the family knew well.

He wanted to cook the foods that they'd grown up loving. For appetizers, he chose items like fresh rice-paper-wrapped spring rolls, fried egg rolls, crispy chicken wings, and small bowls of wonton soup with the available green vegetables (broccoli instead of the mustard greens from the old country and the familiar but milder American green onions and cilantro). For entrées, he wanted to have bun noodle bowls containing soft fermented rice noodles with fresh vegetables to recall spring and summer, even across the cold winter. He filled them with lettuce, carrots, bean sprouts, an assorted variety of fresh herbs like mint and cilantro, grilled meats with crispy edges, all mixed with a light dressing of *nuoc Cham* (fish sauce), sugar water, garlic, a small taste of fresh chili, all balanced with lime juice. He wanted to serve pan-fried pork chops seasoned with lemongrass, brown sugar, and fish sauce, a fried egg, pickled radish and carrots, and thin slices of cucumber on plates of broken rice. These were everyday dishes the family loved.

Most important, though, he and the whole family agreed, they had to serve *pho*. It was the national dish of Vietnam, the everyday person's food, and the most common among the noodle soups connecting the Southeast Asian refugee groups coming into the area: the Laotians, the Hmong, the Cambodians, and the Vietnamese all loved their *pho*. While the family was confident that with exposure and education, more established Minnesotans would grow to love the flavorful, comforting dish, they knew that without the patronage of the other refugee groups, the restaurant couldn't survive in a landscape where who they were and the foods they ate remained foreign and questionable.

The family had their own special recipe, their special blend of spices. While *pho*, rice noodles in a rich broth, usually made of long-simmered beef bones, seasoned with charred onions, ginger, spices such as cinnamon, star anise, black peppercorn, and coriander, is fairly typical, theirs would not be. Their dish would be garnished with a variety of meats from tripe to meatballs, from fresh, thinly sliced beef to pieces of soft-boiled tendon. Each bowl would be topped with sliced green onions and cilantro and accompanied with a side of fresh bean sprouts, sprigs of Thai basil, wedges of lime, and slices of jalapeño peppers. They were confident that most Vietnamese folks would love what they had to offer.

However, the reality was that they were not dealing with a predominantly Vietnamese clientele. While most Vietnamese eat their *pho* with the vegetables, not disturbing the broth, dipping their meats into a combination of hoisin sauce and sriracha hot sauce in a side dish on the table, the refugees who came from Thailand, influenced by the Thai palette, liked to add in additional condiments such as sugar, fish sauce, soy sauce, hoisin sauce, oyster sauce, sriracha sauce, hot chili and garlic oil, and sliced chili peppers in vinegar. Some asked for crushed roasted peanuts in their noodle dishes. Thankfully, the Truong family were fast learners, able to accommodate the different communities who came to their establishment.

By 1984, the restaurant was ready for its grand opening. After consulting with Mrs. Truong and his brothers, Mr. Truong announced that the restaurant would be named after the infamous Caravelle Hotel in Ho Chi Minh City. While he had never been inside the grand hotel, he had admired it from the outside. The hotel was an impressive ten-story building built in 1959 by a Vietnamese architect who'd been trained at École Supérieure des Beaux Arts in Hanoi. In the 1960s the hotel housed only the wealthiest political officers, businessmen, and great foreign powers in the country: the Australian embassy, the New Zealand embassy, and the Saigon bureaus of NBC, ABC, and CBS. When Saigon fell in 1975, the Caravelle was taken over by the government and renamed Doc Lap Hotel, or Independence Hotel. It was not until 1998, long after the Truongs' Caravelle Restaurant was born on their corner of University Avenue, that the hotel was relaunched once again as the Caravelle. For Mr. Truong, the naming of the restaurant was a victory, both personal and historical.

The Caravelle Restaurant did well for the Truongs. It successfully attracted the array of Southeast Asian refugees who were settling in the area and many of the people who worked with them: refugee resettlement workers, teachers, local churches who'd sponsored families, and others. The restaurant was the first place of work for many of the children as well as the place that fed them. In fact, after the restaurant closed for the day, when the family was too exhausted to go home, too aware that soon a new workday would dawn, Mr. and Mrs. Truong's five children used to study and sleep in their father's basement office, a darkened room in an unfinished space. They took their pencils and pens to its walls. They wrote misspelled American swear words for fun. They drew pictures of each other. They played games like hangman and tic-tac-toe on the darkened walls. The Truong children all became young men and women in that place. The restaurant allowed Mr. and Mrs. Truong to send all their children to college. It became part of the positive change that city planners and the residents of Frogtown had been hoping for, but could not have designed: the resurgence of University Avenue.

The Caravelle and countless other ethnic restaurants and

shops that opened up on University Avenue in the 1980s, 1990s, and 2000s turned the avenue from an abandoned, dying street into a vibrant enclave of diverse businesses that served their communities and attracted others. Individuals from the different refugee groups bought the old buildings and renovated them as they knew how, to make room for grocery stores, tailoring shops that made traditional clothes, bakeries that sold the breads they knew from different parts of the world, and butchers that catered to specific groups, such as halal meats for Muslims and a Mexican carnicería with common cuts for their dishes. Wealthier refugees bought the bigger buildings and rented them out as smaller spaces to industrious men and women who wanted to try their hand at working for themselves. A Hmong dentist bought an old car dealership and set up his office in there, then rented part of it to a Hmong restaurateur who wanted to open up a Thai restaurant. There was still room, so he rented out the remaining space to a Hmong chiropractor who wanted to have his own practice. Business developers saw what was going on, noticed the traffic that the newcomers were bringing in, and reinvested on the stretch, bringing box stores, a new public library, and housing initiatives.

By the time Hai left for college, the University Avenue of his youth was gone. Like his father, Hai felt responsible for the trajectory of his family's story. He was the first person in their family to gain a college education. While Mr. and Mrs. Truong had always said, "We want you to be happy," Hai felt a need to show them how lives could be lived in America away from the endless demands of a family restaurant.

After college, Hai found a job in the corporate world as an

analyst. In his suit and tie, Hai made good money. His parents were proud. He represented the successful journey they'd taken after leaving their country, working hard in the restaurant business, raising children who wouldn't have to work with their hands for a living. However, what they didn't know and what Hai himself was only slowly realizing was, he was unhappy. Hai was drinking away the money he earned as fast as he was earning it. He was depressed. He missed the hustle and the bustle of a restaurant. One April Fools' Day Hai told his boss that he was done with corporate America.

It took Hai another ten years before he could tell his mother and father that he wanted to start a restaurant, and asked if they would help him.

In their fashion, Mr. and Mrs. Truong went about teaching Hai everything they knew, all the places where the corners could be cut, who to hire and how to arrange work in a restaurant to make it efficient and cheap. While Hai understood where they were coming from, it wasn't what he wanted. Hai wanted to build on the legacy that his parents had made in America, not just re-create it.

Hai listened and learned from his parents knowing that what he would do would be different. From the beginning, Hai wasn't just concerned about making a go in the restaurant business; he wanted his restaurant and his business to contribute actively to the lives of the people who worked for him, the people who ate his food, the community that had raised him. He wanted to rebrand *pho* and *bun*, the dishes from his youth, by using the best in what the local food producers had to offer rather than the most affordable ingredients. The more Mr. and Mrs. Truong heard of Hai's ideas, the more skeptical they became. Where would he make money if he was going to invest it all back into the restaurant? Where did he want to place this restaurant with the best ingredients? Certainly not on University Avenue?

That was exactly what Hai wanted. His parents were skeptical but they agreed if that was what he wanted to do with his life, they would help him. In fact, it was Mr. Truong who suggested that Hai buy the old Caravelle Restaurant from his aging aunt who had taken over the family enterprise and renamed it Pho Anh. Mr. Truong's sister was getting too old to manage the operation. Her fingers, once straight and strong, were now bent and red. Beyond her age, there was talk of University Avenue changing in a big way once again. The city planners wanted a return to the old trolley; this time it would become a light-rail. She was afraid of what such a change would do. The aunt was eager to sell the place to her nephew for a fair price.

Hai got married the same year he opened his restaurant, in 2007. He completely remodeled the place. One of the first things he did was to seal the door his father had made in the front of the restaurant; he opened the original door in the corner. Hai knocked down all the walls in the restaurant so he could see the structure for what it was, unmarred by the story of how new refugees had to survive with what had been there before them. He tore down the stained tiled ceiling and installed an authentic tin one. He secured a liquor license and made the bar himself out of expensive, solid wood, stocked with the finest selection he could afford, saving room for the local brews he knew were bubbling away nearby. Hai furnished the place with solid wood tables and chairs that he himself wanted to sit at and eat on. He demolished the old kitchen and had a brand-new one put in with ventilation and equipment of the highest quality. He was determined to open an eatery that would attempt to do what no refugee-owned restaurant on University had attempted: to attract people with money, individuals who could afford to make their food decisions based on their understanding of local and global economies.

Hai hired the best people he could find, individuals who wanted to grow in the restaurant business, people who wanted to work competitively for competitive pay. In his kitchen, full of stainless steel, he tried recipe after recipe, following his dream of using the best local ingredients to create the most flavorful dishes without fear of not being authentic enough. He had stodged and dined at the finest restaurants in the Twin Cities and elsewhere looking for ideas, trying to satisfy his increasingly complicated tastes. Hai refused to cut corners. He used no instant soups or easy sauces. Hai gave the restaurant everything he had to give, he made it everything he loved about what a local restaurant could be: a place full of local brews, food made with local produce, operated by local people.

Hai named his restaurant Ngon Bistro. He had traveled to France and, each time he had entered a bistro there, he was surprised to find that it was more familiar than different. The food reminded him of the Vietnamese food he'd grown up with in his home. He liked the bistros for their clean and their calm, the good food they prepared served with professionalism but no fanfare. Hai wanted to replicate that. At the same time, he didn't want to lose himself or give up any part of his identity. Hai wanted to be Vietnamese and to stamp this restaurant with Minnesota, this state that had been his home since he was five years old. Of course, he was also focused on stamping Minnesota with himself, an ethnic Chinese Vietnamese boy who had been born far away, who'd come here as a refugee child, grown up with overworked parents, feeding people because he loved them.

The one thing Hai did not change in the building was his father's basement office. He couldn't do it. Those old walls with the bad words, hand-drawn images, and the games he and his siblings had played together. Hai wanted a reminder of who he had been, who they had been, and what they had all been together: newcomers making a go at a new life.

◆

All his life, Hai has had a tendency to let his mind block out all the mean things, the unsavory things, the undelicious elements of everything. He does not want to remember Vietnam despite the fact that he was already five when his family fled the country. All he remembers is that they were able to leave together. He has no desire to remember the early years of being in America when the family survived on public assistance.

There are no details in his memory of the racial fights he was engaged in when the white kids didn't like the fact that there was a sullen Vietnamese boy in their class with his head of dark hair and matching eyes. However, the faces of the few white kids who fought with him to even the odds, he'll never forget. There was the boy with shaggy brown hair, holes in his jeans, and freckles across his nose; then another boy who was so tall and big he doubled the size of Hai himself, his hair cut like a man in the military, ears sticking out like butterfly wings on the sides of his head.

Hai doesn't want to remember the prostitutes positioned on the corners of old University Avenue. Instead, he focuses on the image of his wife standing outside their restaurant, declaring to the world, "This. This is my corner now." Hai understands his predicament well as a refugee child, one who came here young enough to garner the skills to survive and to succeed but is also chased by the ghosts of old.

While Hai grew up in the restaurant with Mr. and Mrs. Truong at the helm, he lived with his paternal grandmother. She, in fact, raised him.

It started in the early 1980s when Mr. Truong was buying the building to house the restaurant. Hai was not part of the decision. It was an expectation so he complied.

The boy and his grandmother moved all over the Cities in search of a neighborhood and a school that could accommodate their lives. They lived in a house in Minneapolis, then in a small apartment two blocks from the restaurant, and then in an old apartment on 7th Street on the east side of the city, flooded with refugees from Laos. Hai knew his cousins the same way he knew his siblings. He grew up living with his aunts and uncles whenever his grandmother found herself living with them—which happened every couple of years. In each place, Hai was the first son of the first son, so everyone loved him and treated him with a deference. And yet in those years with his grandmother, their lives were much like University Avenue: messy, always changing.

Hai believes, like his father, that "the past is only useful if it allows us to move forward."

◆

Ngon Bistro became a success. White folk with money entered its doors enthusiastically. Other folk, curious, came and tasted from its menu. The food was good. The bar was excellent. The environment was different than the other establishments on the avenue. The restaurant stood out, and Hai along with it. Local newspapers came asking for the family's story, Hai's philosophy on food and business, the particular inspirations for his dishes, dishes not traditionally found in a Vietnamese family restaurant. In 2020, Hai was nominated for a James Beard Best Chef Midwest Award.

◆

When Hai and his wife were pregnant, Hai made a decision to keep his child close. Before the baby was born, Hai did everything he could to ensure that he'd have time to be with his child. Hai wanted to make sure that he would have the time to spend with his child outside of work, that he could keep his son close to him.

When Donald Trump won the presidency in 2016, Hai was downstairs in his father's old office. All of a sudden he felt the past reaching out its hands, not for him this time, but for Khanh, his son. Hai had looked and sounded different. Khanh did not look or sound different in the same ways but it was Hai's blood and legacy that flowed through the boy's thin body, his own complicated composition. Hai was 75 percent ethnic Chinese. Mr. Truong speaks two dialects of Chinese. While Hai could no longer speak Chinese, all his life he'd looked Chinese in a Vietnamese life. Each time he'd moved to a different school, he became an Asian boy in a pool of two or three. Now there was Khanh, who didn't look Chinese or Vietnamese, or white, although his mother is white. Hai had believed that he had survived the race fights so Khanh wouldn't have to. Would the boy have to fight? Would he even know how?

Khanh had playdates. He had neighborhood friends. He had cousins who adored him, a life built around his needs. Unlike Hai. Hai, who had been Mr. Truong's second-in-command, played his expected role as living companion to his grandmother and somehow managed to carve a life that was not so expected.

Who had taught him how to fight? Was it his father whose life was lived in the restaurant, always balancing numbers and attitudes and needs? Was it his grandma who loved him but did not shower him with affectionate words or gestures, just her beloved rice cakes and pork steamed buns? Was it himself? A boy with hair in his face, looking and taking notes with his eyes? Or was it University Avenue? This place that had been old but was made new again and again by the people who came to the stretch, saw something of the future in the past, and did the hard work of making others believe? No. It was the restaurant itself, the old Caravelle and then the new Ngon Bistro, these places that proved they could provide what was necessary for a man, a family, a person to dream of better times, to live away from the past but remain part of it.

In 2016, Hai wiped away his own tears. He traced the words he'd written on the darkened walls as a boy, the F, the U, and the K. Hai decided that no matter who was president, no matter the mood of the country, his son would survive because he had. Whether his father wanted to or not, Mr. Truong had never been able to shield his son from the demands of life in America, from the pressures of having to survive against all odds.

—Hai Truong

14

Never Going Home Again

MINNESOTA IS NOW just this place in my brain where there is snow on the ground, tall white men in white lab coats, their needles sinking deep into my legs, through skin and muscle. It is a wet, cold place full of even colder people: a man and a woman who chose to send their child on vacation far from them for years and never say anything on the phone like "I'm sorry" or "I love you" or "We sent you away because it was the only thing we could do." Instead, they want to talk like this is normal, they want me to tell them, "I'm okay," and "School is great," and "I'm happy."

I was born to Cambodian refugee parents. I never thought that I myself would experience life as a refugee, someone who can't return home because I am understood as a threat to who the locals are and want to be.

The day my father told me that I was going on vacation with Grandma, Auntie, Uncle, and my cousins was one of the best days of my childhood. I had never been on vacation anywhere. Everyone had always said that it was too hard to take me and my wheelchair and my medications, that things could go wrong and too many places weren't wheelchair accessible. But out of nowhere, my father told me the good news.

I was a child with a round face, eyelashes so long that they fanned across my field of vision. I had a wide mouth full of teeth. I can see my face then: a child's picture of happiness.

My father's face was thin. He wore thick glasses. A balding man with a scraggly beard, his mouth was a replica of my own except it was not smiling; he was grimacing, as if he was in pain.

My mother didn't say anything about the vacation. She had her back to me the whole day. All I saw were her rounded shoulders, sloping toward her arms, the curls at the back of her head the product of a perpetual perm. In the kitchen, she looked out the window. In the living room, she sat in front of me and looked at the television. Beside me, she looked away from me. All my life, when my mother spoke to me at all, she began with, "It is a pity."

I was a pity. Everyone in the community, my aunts, my uncles, and my cousins, all felt this way. Even my three older brothers, who joked and talked with me, thought it was pitiful that I was born the way I was.

I was born with muscular dystrophy. I've known this since I was three years old.

It would have been easier for everyone, including myself, if I had been born in Cambodia and had lived through Pol Pot and was made this way through war. But I was born after the war in a new country in a life that was supposed to be easier for everyone, only I wasn't easy. I lived as a reminder of how life could be hard—even away from war.

Refugees do not know the moment their lives are going to change forever.

That day, the sun was coming in through the windows. My father and I were in the living room. I was in my wheelchair looking at the television screen. My father was seated at his usual place, at the end of the old sofa, on the edge of its sagging cushion. He was leaning toward me, his elbows on his knees, fingers laced together. He said, "Son, you're going on vacation to California with your auntie, uncle, the cousins, and Grandma. Remember my sister and her husband who used to live here? They're in California now."

The school year was nearly over and I knew the endlessly long summer days were coming.

I asked, "Have you gotten me a plane ticket?"

My father answered, "You are going in a car, a van, Auntie and Uncle's blue Plymouth."

I know I screamed with excitement. I reached for him, to hug him. He wrapped me in his arms and sniffed my hair, held me closer than he'd ever held me.

◆

In the van, I was placed in the back row with some luggage around me. The food was beside me in a brown bag and a cooler. The adults packed food for the entire trip. The smell, the salt of the fish sauce, the sweetness of brown sugar, and the scent of garlic oil teased my nose the whole ride.

There were three children on the trip. My older cousin was eight or nine. My younger one was five. I was seven. I could read already. I spent the majority of the drive reading to my little cousin. The drive to California took three days. It was a long time—even for a kid who had lots of experience sitting and being on wheels.

Auntie was as nice as they came. Although she was my mother's sister, she was softer toward me than my mother. She could bear to talk to me and look me in the eye without pain or pity. She laughed and checked in on me from time to time from her seat in the front, beside Uncle, the silent driver, calling back, "Tommy, you holding up back there?"

I knew she could see me from the vanity mirror of her sunshade. I nodded at her from my place in the back of the van.

Uncle had married into the family. He was a quiet, intimidating man who looked at everything and everyone around him with suspicion. The only expression he carried on his face was concern. His body was stiff. Auntie said that Uncle used to be a relaxed guy; she said that Pol Pot had done this to him. Whatever Pol Pot had done, it was clear that Uncle was ready for anything, and I knew that I wasn't, so I stayed off his radar as much as I could.

Grandma had no smell. She didn't chew betel nuts, use tiger balm, or like one particular dish over another. Grandma bathed but held no hint of sweet-smelling soaps or floral shampoo, and she wore no perfume. Her skin was gray like the Minnesota winter. Deep lines were carved into her face, suggestions of a life full of laughter and tears. She spent much of her time on the road trip drinking water, washing away whatever smell she might have had. Occasionally, she exclaimed over something on the side of the road—"I'm finally seeing the world!"—to no one in particular. I wished she had a smell that would tell me she was close by.

My little cousin was cute. Although I was in a wheelchair, he looked up to me. He liked the jokes I told.

"When do you reach your final height?"

"When you die."

He would shake his head as if I'd said the most incredible thing in the world. The kid made me smile on that trip.

We must have looked odd. A Khmer family with an old woman and a boy in a wheelchair, getting out of the car to use the bathrooms but never buying food. I was used to people staring so it wasn't a big deal. We kept the exchanges short. "Hi, where is the bathroom?" Nods of gratitude. We tried to show more of what we felt than say it. Somehow it was easier for people to see Khmer folk than to hear us. Even as a kid, I knew this.

The rest stops were awesome. They were the highlight of the trip. The best part about them: the fresh air. The closer we got to California, the dryer the air became. The rest of the family stretched their legs at the rest stops. I stretched my lungs.

◆

The California heat was overwhelming. I had on a hoodie and I wanted Auntie to take it off. My skin felt itchy. The uneaten food had started to smell and it bothered my stomach.

From her mirror, Auntie could see I was getting agitated.

She called back, "Be patient, Tommy. I'll come and help you when the car stops."

I rolled my eyes because I had no choice but to be patient. Unlike other kids, my tantrum options were low.

I had imagined someplace by the ocean, but I saw no coastline on our way to California. To my cousins' and my own disappointment, the car stopped before a small one-story house in a busy part of a flat town. Men and women in thin jackets, who obviously were not from Minnesota, walked by, looking cool, with their chins high. When the family finally unloaded me on the busy sidewalk, people made room for my chair. I saw that the cement below me was cracked and uneven. There was chewed-up, stepped-on gum, cigarette butts, straw wrappers, and other bits of small trash on the ground. I saw my first garbage bushes: plastic bags, food wrappers, and empty cans tucked in the thickets like fruit. We all waited on the sidewalk as Auntie and Uncle approached the front door of the small house.

I missed my father a lot in that moment and wished he'd come along with us.

♦

Once, my father and I had gone on a drive together after school. It was a splendid autumn day in Minnesota, perfect hoodie weather. The sun was high and the sky was blue and the clouds were white and scattered in the direction of the wind. My father had picked me up from school. My teacher had gotten me ready, helping to secure my backpack to my wheelchair. When she saw my father walking our way, she said, "Mr. Sar, you have a smart one here. Tommy is a witty kid."

The lines around my father's eyes fanned out with his smile. He said, "Yes, he is a smart kid."

After school, my father drove us in our old white and brown Buick, bought used but new to us, through the nice neighborhoods in Minneapolis. I watched the back of my father's head and the big houses on either side of the street from my place behind him. All the houses looked empty, but their lights were on, so we knew they were not empty, just way bigger than the people inside could fill. The trunks of the trees lining the streets were brown, a nice contrast against the grass still green from summer. The leaves were falling off the ash trees, raining yellow color like in a Korean drama. My father and I could have starred in a Korean drama about a loving father and his chill, wheelchair-bound son that day.

I told my father that fall is my favorite season in Minnesota. I told him I loved the smell of the dry leaves in the air. I asked him what his favorite time of the year was when he was a boy like me.

My father told me that when he was a boy in Cambodia, he loved the ending of the monsoons and the beginning of the dry season. He said the grass and trees were at their lushest then. The earth gave off its own smell, not at all like dry leaves, but a smell like the dirt itself was blooming.

I asked my father if he ever thought he'd leave Cambodia when he was a boy.

He asked me if I thought I'd ever leave Minnesota.

We both shook our heads no.

When we got to our house in Minneapolis, we both let out a sigh. It'd been a nice drive. Home was where we needed to be but neither of us really wanted to go in. Except there was no time to linger, because our front door opened, and we saw one of my father's best friends waving.

My father carried me inside. His friend greeted us by opening the screen door and then leading the way into the living room. My father set me up in front of the television. He went to the kitchen and grabbed beers for his friend and himself.

His friend, a short guy who dressed like a teacher from the past, in a button-up shirt and slacks, asked, "Hey, Tommy, what do you want to be when you grow up?"

I looked at my father when I answered. "A naval engineer, like my father was in Cambodia."

The friend clapped me on the shoulder. "Good boy."

My father said, "Tommy is really smart at school. He can be anything he wants. A lawyer. A judge. Anything at all."

Just for fun I asked, "What if I want to be an astronaut one day?"

My father laughed out loud. "Then you will be an astronaut one day."

We both knew there were no astronauts in wheelchairs, but I liked that he said I could be one. He always tried to support everything positive I had to say about myself or the world we lived in.

◆

Auntie and Uncle stood at the door listening for voices we couldn't hear. From the sidewalk, I could see that the grass on the square lawn was already yellow in places and drying up along the edges of the sidewalk. I thought it would be a cool science experiment to measure the temperature of the grass near the concrete and then in the center of the yard. The sound of a door slamming from inside the house turned my attention away from the lawn. I noticed that the window curtains were old bed sheets, repurposed. I looked away and tried not to judge.

My father's childless sister and her husband opened the door together. They were the same height. Both were thin. They had curly hair that was more gray than black. She wore a black shirt with brown flowers on it. He wore a mechanic's outfit. They greeted Auntie and Uncle, but I could see that their eyes were trained on me.

I tried not to wrinkle my nose as they moved close to me and started petting me. My California Uncle smelled like car oil and WD-40 (he'd tell me later that he purposely sprayed his hands with WD-40 so that his boss at the car-repair shop would smell him and think he was always working). I let the California Aunt help me out of my hoodie and fan me with her hands.

It turned out that the house wasn't theirs alone. They shared it with another Khmer family, a mother and a father, their two children, and a dog. They pointed to the yellow spots on the lawn and told us that it was the result of dog pee. Inside, the California Aunt and California Uncle had a single bedroom with a television set. They had set up a bed for me near the only window in their room. The rest of the visiting family would sleep in the living room on mats. I felt like an extra-special guest.

We stayed with the California Aunt and California Uncle and the family they lived with for a few days. The adults visited. We ate good food, not everyday chicken and pork family dishes but the more expensive food that people made for guests, like fish soup in sour tamarind broth and big shrimps fried with garlic in a caramelized soy sauce. The cousins played outside on the square lawn with the other children and their dog. The children, once they had gotten comfortable with me and my wheelchair, were friendly but they didn't know what I could and couldn't do so they didn't invite me to play with them. I spent most of my time sitting by the window in the small living room looking outside at the cars filing past the house. I enjoyed seeing the pickup trucks with men and boys sitting in the open back—something I'd never seen in Minnesota. I imagined myself with them on the truck beds, feeling the wheels run over the road, the bumps and jumps. By the end of day five, I was ready to return home to my family.

But the aunt and uncle who had brought me decided to take us kids to Mexico for a few days, since we were on vacation. It didn't make sense to be so close to another country and not go, they said. When was the next time the kids would get to come back to California? The adults had come here from Cambodia, but my cousins and I had never been outside of the States. Grandma didn't want to come with us. She wanted to spend time with California Aunt and California Uncle. I was excited to go somewhere else. The thought of being able to say to my classmates in the fall, "This summer we crossed the border into Mexico from California," sounded really cool to me.

We got in the blue Plymouth van and waved good-bye to the group standing outside the little house with the spotted lawn. Mexico was not as different from America as I'd hoped, despite the excitement of entering into a different country through a checkpoint. We got there late afternoon and ate the food the California Aunt had packed for us. Auntie and Uncle checked us into a hotel that smelled like cigarette smoke. By the time the sun had settled over the horizon, we were all tucked in for bed. My cousins slept on a sheet on the carpeted floor. I got the couch and the comforter although it was hot and I didn't need it. Auntie and Uncle took the bed with the pillows. In the morning, we began our first and last day as tourists. We got up early and ate the cold rice and meat leftover from yesterday. We got ready and headed outside, loaded the car, then joined the groups of tourists on the busy street admiring men with colorful sombreros and women holding painted maracas in green, blue, red, and yellow with designs like cacti and chilis. When the sun grew hot, we stood in the shade of the buildings and watched a lot of tourists buying colorful trinkets and treats. I don't even remember what we ate or if anyone bought anything. The dust of Mexico made the biggest impression on me. I had to squint my eyes the whole time, so I saw the country from beneath the fan of my lashes. Auntie took a few photos of us kids smiling and struggling to keep our eyes open in the sun. When Uncle decided we had experienced enough of

Mexico, they carried me to the car, everybody else climbed in, and we headed back.

It was not until the border crossing back into the United States that things got eventful. Everyone had a passport but me. I had no paperwork at all. I could hear Auntie and Uncle talking quietly to each other. I could hear the silence stretch between their words. My little cousin asked if they were going to have to leave me behind. I rolled my eyes but inside me there was a sinking feeling. How come the adults hadn't thought about getting me a passport when everybody else had one? Surely, if I were left behind in Mexico, I would die. I tried to swallow my fear and act brave. That meant I had to hold my chin up the whole time and look around as if I was just bored. I tried not to watch Auntie or Uncle too closely. I didn't want them to think I was afraid they would leave me behind. I didn't want to hurt their feelings, because they were the first adults to take me on a real vacation.

When my neck grew tired of holding up the weight of my head, I looked at my shoes. I imagined my toes inside them. I wished I was a normal Cambodian kid with dusty toes. I knew that inside my shoes, inside my socks, my toes were pale and wrinkled, unexposed to the elements, weak because they had never exercised, tired despite the fact that they had not taken me far. I saw my cousins in front of me in the van, kicking their legs, their sandals on the floor, and I saw their toes, which were healthy and brown from the days in the sun. Their feet were dirty and I felt a wave of longing to touch my bare toes to earth that was so deep it made my toes tingle.

I felt Auntie's eyes on me. When I met her gaze, she tried to smile reassuringly but I saw the cloud of worry in her gaze. She turned to Uncle and said, "How about we block him with the luggage and cover him with a blanket, and just cross over and hope no one finds him?"

Uncle answered, "You think you can fool the US government?"

She said, "We have to do something."

He shrugged and parked and they embarked on Auntie's plan to get me back into the country.

Beneath the hot blanket, I could barely breathe. I could hear the cassette tape my aunt and uncle were listening to, a Khmer rock 'n' roll song, the kind my father used to play around the house, Khmer rock 'n' roll that sounded more like old country music. My brothers hated that music, but I didn't. I knew the song well despite my lack of fluency in Cambodian— "Champa Battam Bong," a song about longing for a place. Beneath the hot blanket, sweat and tears started to roll down my face. Afraid to wipe them and move and lose everything in America, specifically Minnesota, I let the river run its course, telling myself if I made it back to the other side of the border, I'd tell everyone about the sweat, never the tears.

When we were safely back in California, in the small house where Grandma, California Aunt and California Uncle, and the other Khmer family with their two children and their dog waited for us, I decided I should be more grateful for the people in my life. I didn't pester anyone. I spent my days watching television in the bedroom I shared with California Aunt and California Uncle. I got used to the smell of car oil and WD-40. They checked in on me at all hours of the day, asking if I was thirsty or hungry, if I needed this or that.

We were in the second week of vacation when Grandma asked me if I liked being in California. It was evening. The

Khmer family and their dog, my aunts and uncles and cousins were all gathered on the small lawn that was now more yellow than green. The adults sat around a charcoal grill while the kids chased the dog for fun. I knew that when the food was ready, they'd bring me a plate. The window was open so the smell of grilled meat and summer night entered the house. From the garlic and scent of slightly burned sugar in the air, I knew they were making *chez sovan*, Cambodian beef sticks, and *poat dot*, Cambodian grilled corn. I could hear the kids laughing, calling to the dog. Grandma and I were in the living room together. She leaned back on a mountain of folded mats and blankets that everyone slept on. She held a plastic cup of water in her hands. Her voice was hushed and serious, in conflict with the mood of the evening. When I didn't answer immediately, she asked again, "Do you like it here in California?"

I said, "Yes, Grandma. This has been wonderful. The California Aunt and California Uncle have been so nice and generous to us all, but especially me."

She was quiet.

I smiled at her.

She took a drink of water from the cup she held with both hands.

Only the lamp in the corner was on. The shadows in the room were reaching for us in the darkness. In the dim lighting, I saw her face, full of wrinkles, turned toward me, looking at me with pity and love, above the rim of her glass.

I asked her, "Aren't you having fun?"

She answered in her usual way. "I have had my fun, Tommy. Don't worry about me. It is I who worry about you."

I must have said, "Yeah, Grandma," because that was what I did back then, agree with everyone's worries about me.

That night, there was a mood of celebration around the meal. The adults reminisced about the good times long ago. The Khmer woman living in the house started talking about how the best deals for rice cookers and other Asian pots and pans were in Chinatown in Los Angeles. She suggested Auntie and Uncle go and buy some before returning to Minnesota. Auntie told her about University Avenue, where there were Asian shops and restaurants, and plenty of pots and pans for sale. The woman laughed. "No, it's nothing like that. I've been to University Avenue. This is way cheaper. Much better. You should take your kids. They'd enjoy it. It is almost like a different country. Way better than University Avenue." I rolled my eyes at their talk. If Chinatown was even more foreign than University Avenue, I didn't care for it. I hated University Avenue, I thought it was too "ethnic"—my slur for everything that was not American. I urged the other children, exhausted from their play outside, to join me for a movie on television.

The next day, early in the morning, before I had woken up, the blue Plymouth van left the little one-story house with the passengers from Minnesota, all except for me. When I got up and I asked where everybody was, California Aunt and California Uncle both said, "They left." I asked when they would return. They said, "We're not sure."

I kept watch at the window that whole day. A part of me thought that maybe they'd gone to Chinatown in Los Angeles. If that was the case, I was glad they hadn't taken me. By evening, though, I started thinking about how they should have taken me, too.

The days passed slowly without the Minnesota contingent. I started thinking that perhaps everybody had gone to Mexico for a last visit before the return to Minnesota. Maybe Auntie and Uncle wanted to take Grandma out of the country so she could say "I'm finally seeing the world" a few more times. If that was where they were, I was thankful they hadn't taken me with them. I didn't know if I could have done another stint under the blanket. Then the days piled up, and I grew uneasy. I tried to move my feet, harder than I've ever tried to before, but to no avail. I couldn't move away from my place by the window.

The routines of the new house grew familiar to me. California Aunt earned a living by taking in sewing from a lady in the neighborhood, sweatshop style. Throughout the day, I could hear the sewing machine go on and off, on and off. In between the run of the machine, she visited me and offered me sweets and little toys she'd purchased from the Asian stores, things for me to hold as I waited for the Minnesota family to return for me. She offered me my favorite food, *yutiao*, crunchy, savory fried donuts shaped like fat, uneven chopsticks. Each time I said, "Thank you for being kind to me," she petted me on the head gently. California Uncle got up early and did not come home until before dinnertime. It became his habit, also, to come and pet me gently on the head like everybody in the house handled the dog.

Within two weeks, a moving van came to the house. On that day, California Uncle had not gone to work. I watched as he opened the door for the men carrying my things: my bed, my other wheelchair, the possessions I had left behind in my room in Minnesota. I stopped being a chill kid that day. I stopped thanking California Aunt and California Uncle, like a guest, for their kindness. I became a refugee, sent far from home.

Later that night, I had California Aunt call my father for me. Our conversation was short.

My father said, "How are you, son?"

I said, "I miss you."

He sobbed. "I miss you, too."

I wanted to lash out at him but I could not.

I had been in this situation before. When I was a kid, my father used to take me to specialists all over the Twin Cities to try to treat my dystrophy. At one place, they gave me electroshock therapy. I remember lying in the bed with electrodes and crying with every shock the doctors administered. One time, I heard my brother, Sam, outside the room talking with our father. Sam asked him, "Why is Tommy crying? What's wrong?" Our father answered in a sobbing voice, "It's to help him. It is not bad. It is to help him." I remember that after I heard the cry in my father's voice, I quieted my own.

I said, "I'll see you soon."

He sobbed once again. "I miss you."

I heard everything I needed in those words, his love, always his love, his optimistic love, a belief that one day we would be reunited. Perhaps when that day came, I could be the astronaut of our dreams and not just the disabled son of a Cambodian refugee struggling to make a normal life for himself and his family in Minnesota. I accepted that we couldn't help what we were, him and me, and that neither of us was ever going to go home again, that we would never return to our favorite seasons.

—TOMMY SAR

15

For My Children

IT STORMED THROUGH the night. Our house shook with the force of the wind. I woke up afraid for the three of you, asleep in your room on the other side of the wall. I got up and walked on creaking floorboards to our bedroom door. In a flash of lightning, I watched your father sleep, an arm raised over his head, neck turned far to the side, a hand on his chest. In the hallway, the door to your room, kept ajar, swung on quiet hinges. The display of lightning outside the hallway window flickered like the start of a movie.

You three slept in your usual line, horizontal on the bed, each on your own pillow, legs and arms tangling with one another's. Yuepheng was at the foot of the bed, close to its edge. He hugged the body pillow that we'd gotten during my first pregnancy—not with you three, but with Baby Jules, the little brother who died inside me at nineteen weeks. Thayeng was in the middle, turned toward Shengyeng, an arm flung across her chest. Shengyeng was at the head of the bed, turned toward the smooth, aged wood. I stood by your bed in the dark, listening to the rhythms of your breathing, holding my own.

In the hallway again, I paused at the window. The string

of lights your father hung in the backyard, behind the garage, between the slate patio that separates the foliage of our yard from our neighbor's, shone in the dark, a swaying series of orbs, miniature planets blazing in a line. In their glow I saw the two metal chairs that your father and I had sat on on our wedding day, the aged ribbons tied to the backs flying in the fierce wind.

The forecast predicted severe thunderstorms on the day of our wedding, August 6, 2011. In fact, storms raged around the Twin Cities except for the small pocket of Phalen Lake Park where we gathered before some five hundred friends and family beneath the trees. The air was thick with moisture, and the sun, peeking between sheets of gray clouds, was hot, but it did not rain. The people drank bottles of water, ate cups of sliced watermelon, and sat in lines or gathered in groups on colorful plastic-woven mats on the hills of green grass around the amphitheater. They all looked down at us sitting on our wedding chairs on the circle of cement. We wore traditional Hmong clothes as your Mimi presided over the Christian portion of our wedding. Mitch, a dear friend, interpreted the scripture your grandmother read from English into Hmong, the language that I want to leave you as a gift but which you are not keen on receiving, at least not yet. The flower bouquet of Oriental hybrid lilies I carried, the most flamboyant among the lilies for their blooms, their colors, and their scents, drew the tears from my eyes, and I cried the whole day, sniffling and blowing my nose, soaking the napkins that friends and family handed me.

Eight years ago, your father and I brought the circles of our lives together for a moment to celebrate our union. The most popular question of the day was, "How did you two meet?"

There was the easy answer. I had just published my first book, *The Latehomecomer.* I had been invited to give a keynote at a Pedagogy and Theatre of the Oppressed Conference at Augsburg University and your father had been advised by his faculty mentors to come and see me, a young Hmong American author. The moment of our meeting is captured on a DVD your father purchased after my talk: I'm standing at the front of the chapel on a stage. Ahead of me, coming up the aisles between the pews of the church, are lines of people, your father among them. Once the people are seated, the camera pans across the crowd and we see the figure of your father slouching in his plaid shirt, rolled to the elbows, a notebook and a pen in his hands. He is frowning, looking at the stage with a furrowed brow. The camera focuses on me. I'm standing as tall as my four feet, ten inches will allow in a white button-up shirt tucked into black pants, long hair pulled back in a loose braid. Halfway through my talk, the camera pans over the crowd again and this time your father is sitting up straight, smiling, eyes sparkling. Your father met me that day, but I didn't meet him until weeks later when he wrote to tell me that what I had said was what he needed to hear, and asked if I would meet with him for coffee. I didn't drink coffee so we met up for lunch. This was the answer we both gave to the most popular question of the day.

The answer neither of us was prepared to give that day is the reason why I am writing these words to you, my children. How did your father and I meet?

Your father and I met because in the late 1950s, long before either of us was born, America entered a war in Southeast Asia, in Laos, a country you know as the birthplace of your Tais Tais and Yawm Txiv. During the war, the Central Intelligence Agency of the United States recruited Hmong people to fight and to die on America's behalf. The Hmong were farmers from the high mountains, trained to tend to the earth. We could not win the fight against the communist soldiers. When Laos fell to communist rule, the Americans left the war with the highest-ranking Hmong military families. They abandoned hundreds of thousands of surviving Hmong to an incoming government that saw them as enemies. My family was one of the families left behind to face genocide. To escape death, your Tais Tais and Yawm Txiv fled across the Mekong River into the refugee camps of Thailand. I was born in Ban Vinai Refugee Camp. I was born with no memories of the war, but stories of how we came to be in this place we couldn't leave, waiting for food to come to us in huge trucks.

Your father and I met because when the Americans left behind what would be called the Indochina Wars, they left millions of refugees in its aftermath. In South Vietnam alone, there were six million refugees, all fleeing persecution. Although most Americans did not know who the Hmong were or that the Americans had been involved in a war in Laos at all, President Gerald Ford signed into law the Indochina Migration and Refugee Act of 1975. This act allowed for the resettlement of refugees from South Vietnam, Laos, and Cambodia. In 1987, my family was able to register as refugees of America's Secret War in Laos through the United Nations High Commissioner for Refugees and apply for resettlement to America.

I was six years old. Your father was eight at the time, living a life in Milwaukee, Wisconsin, with his mother and father, their friends and neighbors. Neither of us could have imagined that our futures would be shared.

Your father and I met because against tremendous odds, some Hmong people survived that war; against incredible odds, some of us resettled to America. I, a refugee child, became a Hmong American girl who became a writer to tell the life story of a wondrous old woman. That writer was invited to give a talk at a conference. Your father, a young scholar, had been in that room and he heard me and wanted to hear more from me.

Because your father and I met, you three are possible. Shengyeng first, with her eyes the color of seagrass. I held her little feet tight in my hand and felt the beat of her heart and my understanding of strength and fragility shifted forever. Thayeng and Yuepheng came together next, one possibility dividing into two, two little boys with matching eyes and noses and mouths, two little ones who came into the world with big voices although their bodies were small. Their cries were like sirens across the quiet landscape of my being and I ran from one to the other, pushed beyond the limits of what I believed my body could deliver. Before your father and I met, all three of you were unimaginable.

My children, you have inherited a world full of war, a world that has always been full of war. You are the children of a refugee. Do not forget this fact.

◆

The people in this book are people from your lives. Fong is an uncle of mine. Siah is a receptionist at the hospital where you were all born. Bayan goes to the college we pass every day when I drop you off at school, on the edge of the high-way, perched over downtown St. Paul. Kaw's son and daughter go to school with you. Awo works at the college perched on the other side of the city, overlooking downtown. Afghanizada is a Lyft driver who stops for coffee at the café blocks from your school. Tommy is my dear friend. Chue is Tais Tais. Majra went to the college I would have gone to if I'd stayed in the Twin Cities. Mr. Michael's daughter went to the college I ended up attending away from the Cities. Saymoukda's picture book rests on your bedroom shelves. Every time we go to Big Daddy's BBQ, we pass by Hai and Khanh's restaurant. Irene sings her songs across these cities. The people in this book are people going through this storm with us all on this very night.

When I was a teenager, reeling beneath the weight of my life and responsibilities, yearning to know the insides of a movie theater, exhausted from imagining what it was like, I told your Yawm Txiv that I didn't want the life I had been granted. I wanted something better. I wanted something more. Your Yawm Txiv told me, "Life will teach you the strength of the human heart, not of its weakness or fragility." His words have stayed with me and fortified my heart in many different moments of hardship. I hope that the stories in this book will do that for you and children everywhere: teach you the incredible strength of the human heart.

◆

The storm that night did not cease; the lightning continued to flash and the sound of thunder echoed.

Later, I dreamed that the creaking house we lived in was the house of our forever. I saw you three, your father, and me in the backyard, gathered around those wedding chairs, beneath the string of sparkling lights. Even in the dream, I knew that houses were not meant to last.

When the paint of the metal chairs has chipped away and the ribbons at their backs have been torn into shreds by the storms of life, remember that somewhere in the unknown world, even without knowing who you would be, I was living for the day you would become, and even when I'm gone, I will look toward the edge of the horizon for your coming.

—KAO KALIA YANG

Logistics of
Refugee Resettlement

A refugee is a person outside of his or her own nationality, unwilling or unable to return to their home country because of a well-founded fear of persecution based on their race, religion, nationality, membership in a particular social group, or political opinion. It is a legal status granted by state governments or the United Nations High Commissioner for Refugees (UNHCR) after careful screening and vetting.

Every October, the president of the United States, in consultation with Congress, sets a cap for the number of refugees we can take in as a country. The State Department is mandated with overseeing refugee resettlement. It works with nine national voluntary organizations that divvy up the humanitarian support for refugees with more than two hundred nonprofit organizations across the nation.

Each refugee is expected to take out a no-interest loan for his or her own flight, with the first installment of the loan to be paid six months after the date of arrival.

When a refugee arrives, each receives a onetime grant of $1,125 from the federal government to be issued by a refugee resettlement agency as it sees fit (generally $50 upon arrival, then $200 to $600 for food and other basic needs, and then the rest held in reserve for housing). Each resettlement agency gets $950 to help each refugee resettle. A refugee has the assistance of a refugee resettlement agency for some ninety days to set up the foundations of a life: secure housing, find jobs, address medical needs, navigate school enrollment, sign up for English-language courses, participate in cultural and safety orientation, and connect with community resources.

Once the period is over, the refugee is expected to survive on his or her own.

Perspectives from
Refugee Resettlement Agencies

Beyond headlines and political speeches, few know who refugees are or how we live. Fewer still gain access to our stories and our lives. We've lost much on our journeys, but the reality is that our stories continue upon our arrival or even as we wait for the possibility of resettlement somewhere.

All of us within this book make our lives in Minnesota, a state that is not known for its diversity, but is thirteenth in the nation for refugee resettlement. Here in Minnesota, we have the highest concentration of Hmong and Tibetan refugees, the biggest Somali, Karen, Burmese, Eritrean, and Liberian refugee populations in the country. All of us live in a state that is predominantly white; non-Hispanic white Minnesotans represent 81 percent of the statewide population.

There are few studies about the racial environment for refugee populations in the state, but Minnesota is one of the worst states in the nation in regard to racial inequality. Minnesota has the highest proportion of people of color, specifically black men, in our prison system; for every 100,000 Minnesotans, there are 1,219 black people incarcerated to 111 whites. Median household incomes for black families are not even half that of white families. The unemployment rate for black people is three times that of whites. Only 21.7 percent of black families own homes compared to 76 percent of white families. The racial environment here, like its climate, can be challenging and deadly.

We also live in a state that has the most diverse neighborhood in the United States. The Phillips neighborhood in south Minneapolis speaks more than one hundred home languages. This state is home to the largest Cambodian Buddhist temple in the country and one of the largest Hindu temples in North America. The University of Minnesota has more Chinese students than any other institution in North America. The Twin Cities has the largest number of Korean adoptees in the nation. We are the site of a $48 million, three-hundred-thousand-square-foot Muslim youth center mosque, the first of its kind in the nation and the largest Muslim mosque in America. The Twin Cities is the most literate city in the country. There are more volunteers to be found here for nonprofit causes than anywhere else. Minnesotans have the highest voting record of any state. We have a Muslim congresswoman and the first Hindu state representative. There are worlds within worlds in this place.

For many of the refugees in this book, our lives here are possible because of the refugee resettlement agencies in the state. There were six in Minnesota: Catholic Charities of St. Paul and Minneapolis, Catholic Charities of Southern Minnesota, International Institute of Minnesota, Lutheran Social Service of Minnesota, Minnesota Council of Churches, and Arrive Ministries. In the course of the writing of this book, Catholic Charities of St. Paul and Minneapolis has stopped its refugee resettlement work due to dwindling funds. Those that remain are just a few of the two hundred nonprofits across the country that handle the humanitarian work of resettling new refugees. Their perspectives are key in understanding the way refugees are welcomed and received across the nation.

According to Ben Walen, division director of refugee services for Minnesota Council of Churches, who started on his professional journey as a young Peace Corps volunteer in Ethiopia, once a refugee arrives, the process is "fast and furious."

He says, "Most refugees are in survival mode. They do not have time or energy to tell their stories; they are too busy learning the ropes: how to communicate, how to operate an American home, how to navigate public transport, feed their families, and stay calm. The first three months of a refugee's life are a blur of new and challenging experiences. If a refugee suffers from post-traumatic stress disorder, the signs don't usually begin to show until after the first three months in America. Most refugee resettlement agencies do not have the funds or personnel to unravel the traumas of war with new refugees."

For Yusuf Abdi, director of refugee services for Lutheran Social Services of Minnesota and a former refugee himself, the resettling of refugees into small towns and communities can be gentler than a move into a big urban center. His own experience of coming to a small community in Pelican Rapids, Minnesota, three and a half hours away from the Twin Cities was a blessed relief. While his parents, other Somali refugees, Bosnian refugees, and the Hispanic population in town worked at the local turkey processing plant, he and his brother had attended the public schools. In the small town, they joined an "international" soccer team with other refugees and immigrants and one Caucasian boy and girl. The team competed for first place in the northwest region of the state tournament, and while they did not take home the championship they came home to a celebration. For Yusuf, "The most critical component of a successful refugee resettlement initiative is to find a place with affordable housing, job opportunities, and a receptive community and school system," and in his experience these places are sometimes quieter, more rural settings.

In a conversation with Bwet Taw, Aimee Barbeau, and Laurie Ohmann, individuals who have worked with Catholic Charities of St. Paul and Minneapolis, for the new refugee "every day is a new beginning." For Bwet, a Karen refugee, the newly arrived refugees often don't know what they are entitled to by law. He was resettled by himself at the age of twenty-two, with limited English, in Kentucky. For the entire first week of his stay in America, he lived in an apartment with no food in the fridge and had no one to call. Bwet knows what many refugee resettlement workers don't know: that often "the refugee feels he is a loser. He has lost everything." As a caseworker now, Bwet's goal is to help new refugees succeed in America from a place of understanding. "Sometimes, I'm the only one talking to them. They compare their home countries to mine. They ask me questions where sometimes I can only answer with 'I don't know'—because it is important for them to hear that they are not the only ones who don't know."

Aimee was the organization's program manager for New American Services. For her, the hardest part of the job was knowing that you're "resettling people into poverty." Laurie, the executive vice president and chief operating officer, believes that resettlement agencies such as Catholic Charities exist as "a voice against the people who make horrific claims and untrue statements about who refugees are and what they bring into this country." Of all the people who enter into the United States of America, refugees go through the most serious vetting. There are no privileges in the refugee process.

For Michelle Eberhard, who used to be the director of refugee arrival services for Arrive Ministries, the most pressing question is, "How do we let people have their own voices in a system that is designed against their stories?"

Acknowledgments

Thank you to the fourteen individuals who have bravely shared their stories with me. Your lives extend far beyond the stories in this collection. Thank you for trusting me and choosing to believe in the heart of this refugee writer. You are the heroes I see in the life we share.

This book benefited from the different refugee resettlement agencies in Minnesota. The work that you have done and continue to try to do allows for these stories to live here.

I want to recognize the generous work of three singular forces for good: Imam Samir Saikali, who invited me into his mosque, the most diverse in Minnesota, and shared from the bounty of his relationships; Dr. Sarah Lucken, pediatrician to countless immigrant and refugee children; and Dr. Tea Rozman Clark, of Green Card Voices, affectionately and respectfully known as the "Balkan hustler," who has connected the threads of humanity in her efforts to build a better world.

In my language, the language of my heart, *ua tsaug ntau.*

About the Author

Kao Kalia Yang is the author of *The Song Poet*, which received the 2017 Minnesota Book Award and was a finalist for the National Book Critics Circle Award, the Chautauqua Prize, the PEN Center USA Literary Award, and the Dayton's Literary Peace Prize. Her previous book, *The Latehomecomer*, also received the Minnesota Book Award and is a National Endowment for the Arts Big Read title. Her debut picture book, *A Map Into the World*, is a Charlotte Zolotow Honor, an ALA Notable Book, Kirkus Best Book of the Year, and a Minnesota Book Award winner. Yang lives in St. Paul, Minnesota.